finger frolics

revised

Compiled by: Liz Cromwell
Dixie Hibner
John R. Faitel

Contributing authors: Rebecca Boynton
Colleen Kobe
Lois Peters
Unknown

Illustrated by: Joan Lockwood

*This book or parts thereof, may not be reproduced in any form
without written permission. All rights reserved.*

Copyright © 1976

Copyright © 1983
ℙ PARTNER PRESS
Box 124
Livonia, Michigan 48152

ISBN 0-933212-10-0

Distributed by: **Gryphon House**
3706 Otis Street
Mt. Rainer, Maryland 20822

INTRODUCTION

Finger Frolics provides the user with a multitude of poems, rhymes, and brief activities to use with young children. These "fingerplays" cover a wide range of topics from fantasy to the very practical. This new edition now includes new topic sections on mythology, magic and make-believe, science, and activity verses in addition to many new fingerplays in the more traditional topics.

Fingerplays are valuable activities for young children because they help the child acquire skills that are essential to their development and learning. Fingerplays help to develop language skills. New words are introduced and correct grammar and usage are modeled. Concepts can be introduced or clarified through the use of fingerplays. Numbers, seasons, and weather are just a few examples. Lessons or units can be introduced or reinforced by the use of appropriate fingerplays. Other objectives include the development of fine motor and gross motor skills through the manipulation of hands, fingers, and body. Auditory memory is improved with the repetition of the rhymes in conjunction with physical action.

Children enjoy the rhyming and the rhythm which promote an enjoyment of poetry. Fingerplays also help the teacher to provide a warm and relaxed atmosphere for the classroom as well as one in which children are involved and learning.

The fingerplays in this book can be used as part of a lesson or as a change of pace between activities. They can be used as a constructive learning experience when there are a few extra moments at the end of a lesson. They can also be used to quiet children after a more boisterous activity. Children should be encouraged to repeat them to each other and to parents and relatives. Fingerplays should be repeated often, but for short periods of time. New ones will be most effective if introduced gradually with an opportunity for practice.

Young children are likely to be more kinesthetic and visual than auditory learners. This is one reason that fingerplays are so important. It will be helpful to provide cues to assist them in remembering the fingerplays. Illustrations in this book or pictures from other sources may be helpful in assisting children to recall the fingerplays. Flannel board cut-outs can be used with some of the rhymes in this book. They will provide another medium for children to manipulate in order to recall the rhymes.

Finally, both the teacher and the child can use their creativity with fingerplays. Different actions can be substituted and new parts added. Pictures can be painted or drawn to illustrate favorite rhymes, or costumes may be worn. Your imagination is the limit.

Have fun with fingerplays!

Liz Cromwell and Dixie Hibner

TABLE OF CONTENTS

self concept

THUMBKIN

Where is thumbkin?
Where is thumbkin? (Hide hands behind back)
Here I am (Bring out one hand)
Here I am (Bring out the other)
How are you today, sir? (Nod one thumb)
Very well, I thank you. (Nod the other thumb)
Run away, run away. (Hide thumbs again behind back)

(Repeat using "Pointer", "Tall Man", "Ring Man", and "Pinkie" instead of Thumbkin)

THUMB MAN SINGS AND DANCES

Thumb man says he'll dance. (thumbs up and nod one)
Thumb man says he'll sing. (nod other thumb)
Dance and sing my merry little thing.
Thumb man says he'll dance and sing.

Pointer says he'll dance.
Pointer says he'll sing.
Dance and sing my merry little thing.
Pointer says he'll dance and sing.

Tall man says he'll dance.
Tall man says he'll sing.
Dance and sing my merry little thing.
Tall man says he'll dance and sing.

Ring man says he'll dance.
Ring man says he'll sing.
Dance and sing my merry little thing.
Ring man says he'll dance and sing.

Pinkie says he'll dance.
Pinkie says he'll sing.
Dance and sing my merry little thing.
Pinkie says he'll dance and sing.

TEN LITTLE FINGERS

I have ten little fingers and they all belong to me. (hands upright)
I can make them do things, would you like to see?
I can shut them up tight; (shut them up into fists)
Or open them wide. (open them wide)
I can put them together, or make them all hide. (close fists together)
I can make them jump high. (swing hands above head)
I can make them go low. (swing hands down low)
I can fold them up quietly and hold them just so. (place in lap)

HEAD AND SHOULDER

My hands upon my head I place
Upon my shoulder, upon my face;
At my waist and by my side
And then behind me they will hide.
Then I raise them way up high
And let my fingers swiftly fly;
Then clap, one—two—three
And see how quiet they can be?

VERY, VERY TALL

I'm very, very tall (stand on tiptoes, arms up)
I'm very, very small (stoop)
Sometimes I'm tall (tiptoes, arms up)
Guest what I am now. (may either stoop or stretch)

MY FINGERS

I stretch my fingers away up high. (lift fingers and stretch)
Until they almost reach the sky.
I lay them in my lap, you see. (fold hands in lap)
Where they're quiet as can be!

STRETCH UP HIGH

Stretch up high.
Stretch down low.
Raise your arms
And away we go.

Make a circle in the air.
Sweep your arm around.
Now the other — do the same
And jump up off the ground.

We like to bend.
We like to stretch.
We make our muscles strong.
Bend, stretch
Bend, stretch
All the whole day long.

First I bend my knees.
Then I stand up tall.
Down, up, down, up
Like a rubber ball.
First I'm short.
Then I'm tall.

MY ARMS

My arms can be all kinds of things,
Make rabbit ears, (Hold arms up along side of head)
And airplane wings. (Hold arms straight out from shoulders)
Or be like the branches of a tree. (Bend arms at elbows)
But best of all,
They're "arms" for Me. (Hold arms out in front)

ME

I can stand away up tall. (Stand on tiptoes)
Then make myself very, very small. (Crouch down)
I can be quiet as quiet can be. (Finger in front of lips)
But here I am, just being ME! (Jump up extending arms)

MANNERS

I have to learn to be polite,
'Cause I'm growing every day.
I'm not a baby anymore,
So there's special things I must say.
I have to say "Please" when I want something,
'Cause that's the polite thing to do.
And when I get the thing I want,
I have to say "Thank You"!

PLEASE & THANK YOU

Some special words we need to know,
And use them every day.
We must say "Please" and "Thank You",
At school, at home, at play.

THIS IS THE WAY WE . . .

(Tune: Mulberry Bush — Play as action suggests)

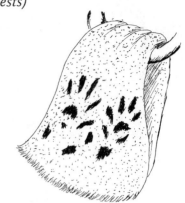

This is the way we wash our hands, etc.
This is the way we comb our hair, etc.
This is the way we brush our teeth, etc.
This is the way we shine our shoes, etc.
This is the way we go to school, etc.

DIRTY HANDS

Dirty hands are such a fright —
See, I washed mine clean and white! (hold hands out, palms up)
Mother says it is quite right
To wash them morning, noon and night.

BRUSHING TEETH

Up and down and round and round (move right pointer up and down, and round
                                    before mouth)
I brush my teeth to keep them sound;
To keep them sound and clean and white (point to teeth)
I brush them morning, noon and night.

BATH TIME

After a bath, I try, try, try
To wipe myself dry, dry, dry. (rub upper arms with hands)
Hands to wipe and fingers and toes. (hold hands out, palms up, then point to toes)
Two wet legs and a shiny nose. (hands on thighs, then point to nose)
Just think how much less time I'd take
If I were a dog and could shake, shake, shake. (shake body)

WASHING MYSELF

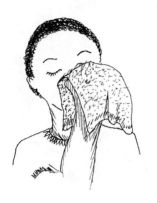

When I was very little and had to wash my face,
I didn't use much water or soap — well, hardly a trace.
I'd fill the bowl with water and dab some on my face.
Here, and here, and here, and here,   (Use pointer finger, touch forehead,
                                        tip of nose, right cheek, left cheek)
And, one other place.   (Touch chin)
I'd go to show my mother. She'd check my face and then,
Because I wasn't clean enough, she'd say, "Go wash again."

GETTING DRESSED

When I wake up in the morning,
I yawn and rub my eyes.   (Yawn, stretch, rub eyes)
Then I hop right out of bed,
And do an exercise.
One, and two, and three, and four.
Reach way high, then touch the floor.   (Stretch hands up then touch floor)
I go into the bathroom,
To wash my hands and face.   (Act out washing hands and face)
I brush my teeth until they shine,   (Brush teeth and hair)
Then comb every hair in place.
Next I put my clothes on,
Fast, but carefully.   (Put shirt over head, pulling up pants)
And when I am all ready,
My Mom is pleased with me.   (Happy look, hands on hips)

POLISHING MY SHOES

This is the way I polish my shoes,
First I put some paper down.
Then I get out the polish,
And dab it all around.
When both my shoes are covered,
And the polish has really dried,
I rub and polish until they shine,
Then I wear my shoes with pride.

EAST AND WEST

This is EAST, and this is WEST. (face east, then west)
Soon I'll learn to say the rest.
This is HIGH and this is LOW, (arms over head, then at side)
Only to see how much I know.
This is NARROW, and this is WIDE. (indicate narrow and wide with hands)
See how much I know beside.
DOWN is where my feet you see. (point to feet)
UP is where my head should be. (hand on head)
Here is my nose, and there my eyes. (point to nose and eyes)
Don't you think I'm getting wise?
Now my eyes will OPEN keep (open eyes wide)
I SHUT them when I go to sleep. (shut eyes, lay head on hands)

SLEEPY HEAD

They call me Little Sleepy Head (point to head)
I yawn at work, I yawn at play.
I yawn and yawn and yawn all day;
Then, I take my sleepy yawns to bed (close eyes, lay head on hands)
That's why they call me sleepy head. (point to head)

GOING TO BED

This little boy (girl) is going to bed (lay pointer in palm)
Down on the pillow he lays his head (thumb acts as pillow)
Covers himself with the blankets so tight (wrap fingers around "Boy")
And this is the way he sleeps all night. (close eyes)
Morning comes, and he opens his eyes (open eyes)
Throws back the covers, and up he flies (open fingers)
Soon he is up and dressed and away (pointer stands straight)
Ready for school and ready for play.

BEING SLEEPY

Sometimes I am sleepy. (Make eyes droopy — then close eyes)
I can hardly stay awake. (Blink eyes several times)
I yawn and rub my eyes. (Rub eyes with fists — give a big yawn)
And give my head a shake! (Shake head back and forth)

OPEN, SHUT THEM

Open, shut them; open, shut them;
Give them a clap.
Open, shut them; open, shut them;
Lay them in your lap.
Creep them, creep them slowly upward
To your rosy cheeks.
Open wide your shiny eyes
And through your fingers peek.
Open, shut them; open, shut them;
To your shoulders fly.
Let them, like the little birdies,
Flutter to the sky.
Falling, falling, slowly falling.
Nearly to the ground,
Quickly raising all your fingers.
Twirling them around.
Open, shut them; open, shut them;
Give a little clap,
Open, shut them; open, shut them;
Lay them in your lap.

RIGHT HAND

This is my right hand; I raise it up high,
This is my left hand; I'll touch the sky,
Right hand, left hand, roll them around.
Left hand, right hand, pound, pound, pound.

RIGHT FOOT AND LEFT HAND

(and reversed)

Stand on right foot,
Raise left hand;

Left hand on right foot —
Straighten and stand.

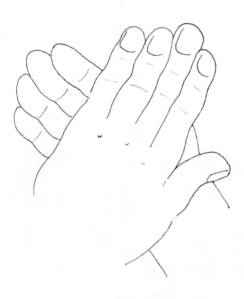

WARM HANDS

Warm hands warm. (rub palms together)
Do you know how?
If you want to warm your hands
Blow your hands now.

8

STRETCH STRETCH

Stretch, stretch away up high; (reach arms upward)
On your tiptoes, reach the sky. (stand on tiptoes and reach)
See the bluebirds flying high. (wave hands)
Now bend down and touch your toes; (bend to touch toes)
Now sway as the North Wind blows. (move body back and forth)
Waddle as the gander goes! (walk in waddling motion back to seats)

HAND ON MYSELF

Hand on myself (point to head)
What is this here?
This is my new noggin, my mother dear.

New noggin, new noggin,
Nick, nick, nick new.
That's what I learned in the school.

Hand on myself (point to eye)
What is this here?
This is my eye winker, my mother dear.

Eye winker, new noggin
Nick, nick, nick new
That's what I learned in the school.

Hand on myself (point to nose)
What is this here?
This is my nose blower, my other dear.

Nose blower, eye winker, new noggin
Nick, nick, nick new
That's what I learned in the school.

Hand on myself . . . .
(Point to mouth eater and repeat.
Next, chin chopper and bread basket.)

READY TO LISTEN

Let your hands go clap, clap, clap; (clap hands three times)
Let your fingers snap, snap, snap; (snap fingers three times)
Let your lips go very round. (make lips round)
But do not make a sound.
Fold your hands and close each eye; (follow action indicated)
Take a breath . . . . . . and softly sigh; (follow action indicated)
Ah — — — — — — — — — —

9

DRAW A PERSON IN THE AIR

To draw a person in the air
I must remember what isn't there.
    (tap temple knowingly)

First I draw an oval face
    (trace outline of head with index finger)
With eyes, nose, and mouth in place.
    (add each in turn)

I draw hair atop the person's head
    (add hair; curly? short? long? etc.)
And then a body with arms outspread.
    (do so)

Legs and feet are last of all.
    (add legs and feet)
Then I erase the invisible wall.
    (make erasing motions, as with
        a chalkboard)

CARING FOR AN ABRASION

If I fall down and hurt myself (rub elbow as if it's hurt)
And no one else is in view, (continue rubbing elbow, look around)
If it hurts, I can cry, but I'm not too scared,
'Cuz I know what to do.

I go to the bathroom (walk a little), turn on the warm water
    ("turn on" water),
And get out a bar of soap; (get soap, rub hands together under
    imaginary faucet)
I ignore the stinging and wash my hurt (rub elbow as if cleaning)
To get all the germs out, I hope.

When I see no more dirt, and the hurt looks clean (inspect elbow),
I'm almost done, and I know it.
I rinse my hurt well (rinse) and pat it dry (pat),
And when mom or dad gets home I show it.

DRESS FOR THE WEATHER!

If you go out without your coat (doff imaginary or real coat)
When the wind is damp and chill, (hug self for warmth)
You'll end up in bed, my friend, (shake finger at observer scoldingly)
Feverish, sneezing, and ill. (look sick, sneeze, wipe sweat from brow)

Wear your boots through snow and mud (don boots)
And during a thunderstorm.
Also wear a waterproof coat and hat (don)
To keep yourself dry and warm.

I STARTED MY LIFE

I started my life
In mother's womb. (pat tummy)
It's warm and dark
Like a cozy room. (hug self)
I started small (place hands close together)
But then I grew (separate hands by wide margin)
'Til I was so big
Mom knew I was due. (trace outline of large tummy)
And so I was born
And my family was glad (smile; clasp hands to heart)
Mom and Dad for me (point to self)
And me for Mom and Dad. (spread arms to embrace)

WHEN I AM . . .

When I am sad, I want to cry. (rub eyes)
When I am proud, I want to fly. (extend arms outwards, veer)
When I am curious, I want to know. (scratch head, puzzled, wave hand
                           as if to teacher)
When I am impatient, I want to go. (cross arms, tap foot)
When I am bored, I want to play. (yawn, look around . . .)
When I am happy, I smile all day. (grin)
When I am shy, I want to hide. (peer over shoulder with back to audience)
When I'm depressed, I stay inside. (rest jaws on fists)
When I am puzzled, I want to shrug. (shrug)
When I am loving, I kiss and hug. (hold arms out and draw in,
                           as if embracing someone)

GROWING UP

When I was just a baby,
I didn't know how to walk.
I could only crawl like this.   (Crawling around)

When I was just a baby,
I didn't know how to talk.
I could only cry like this.   (Waa-waa)

Now I'm this big.   (Raise hands over head)
And I go to school every day.
I know how to do many things,
To walk, and talk, and play.

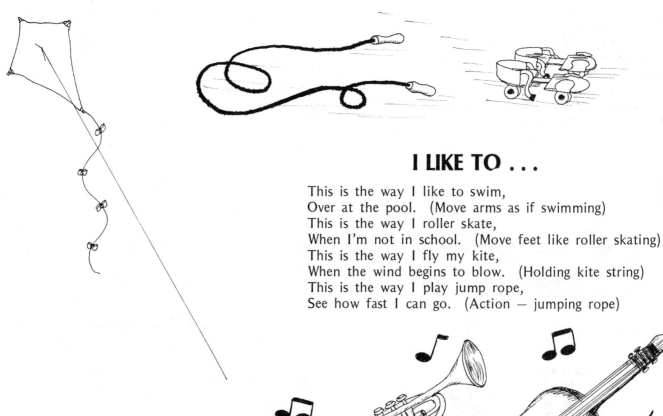

I LIKE TO . . .

This is the way I like to swim,
Over at the pool.   (Move arms as if swimming)
This is the way I roller skate,
When I'm not in school.   (Move feet like roller skating)
This is the way I fly my kite,
When the wind begins to blow.   (Holding kite string)
This is the way I play jump rope,
See how fast I can go.   (Action — jumping rope)

IF I COULD PLAY . . .

If I could play the piano,
This is the way I would play.   (Move fingers like playing piano)
If I had a guitar,
I would strum the strings this way.   (Holding guitar and strumming)
If I had a trumpet,
I'd TOOT to make a tune.   (Like tooting a horn)
But, if I played a drum,
I'd go BOOM, BOOM, BOOM.   (Like playing a drum)

TABLE MANNERS

I watch my table manners,
I sit up nice and straight.
I say, "Please pass this"
and "Please pass that"
And "Please put some on my plate."
I don't talk when my mouth is full,
Nor do I gulp my food.
My mother is very proud of me,
When my manners are good.

LISTENING AND OBEYING

I try to listen and obey,
All the things the teachers say,
Like being quiet and paying attention,
And then I can follow the directions.
I'll try to do all the things I should,
My teacher (mother, father) will be proud of me
For trying to be good.

BEING KIND

I want to be kind as I can be,
With all my friends and family.
I'm not going to punch or hit or shove,
I'll treat them with kindness
And with love.

These are important things to learn,
To wait in line to take my turn.
Not to push or pull someone's hair,
But, with hands to myself,
Stand quietly there.

FRIENDS

I like my friends,
So when we are at play,
I try to be very kind,
And nice in every way.

ACTION GAMES

ALL OF ME

See my eyes. (Point to eyes)
See my nose. (Point to nose)
See my chin. (Touch chin)
See my toes. (Touch toes)
See my waist. (Hands on waist)
See my knee. (Touch a knee)
Now you have seen all of me! (Raise arms)

I CAN HELP

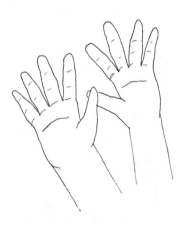

I have two hands to work with. (Hold your hands in front — palms up)
See what they can do.
Brush my hair. (Run hand over hair)
Brush my teeth. (Pretend brushing teeth)
And even tie my shoes. (Bend down as though tying shoes)
I can help my mommy make the bed (Smooth bed)
and sweep the floor. (Sweep floor)
I can carry groceries when we go to the store. (Holding groceries)
And when we get our work done. (Wipe brow — say Whew!)
We have a little treat.
Cookies and a glass of milk,
Are very good to eat. (Rub tummy like "yum-yum")

TAP, TAP

Point your toe. Go tap, tap, tap. (Tap toe)
Press your fingers. Snap, snap, snap. (Snap fingers)
Make your hands go, clap, clap, clap. (Clap hands)
Now it's time to take a nap. (Put hands together, lay head on hands)

QUACK, QUACK

Now I'm up. (Stand up) Now I'm down. (Squat down)
See me waddle all around. (Waddle around)
Put my hands behind my back. (Hands on waist behind back)
Like a duck I'll say, "Quack, quack." (Quack like a duck)

FIVE LITTLE CHILDREN

Five little children on a sunny day,   (Hold up right hand)
One had to take a nap,
There were only four at play.   (Bend down little finger)
Four little children playing a game of ball,
One had to leave when mother gave a call.   (Bend down next finger)
Three little children tried to climb a tree.   (Hold up three fingers)
One went home when he scraped his knee.   (Bend down next finger)
Two little children making a big mud pie,   (Hold up two fingers)
One went home when he got mud in his eye.   (Bend down next finger)
Only one little child playing all alone.   (Hold up thumb)
There was a loud clap of thunder,   (Clap hands together)
And he ran home.

GOING FISHING

When I go fishing down at the brook,   (Hold fishing pole over shoulder)
I put a wiggly worm on my hook.   (Put wiggly worm on hook)
I toss it in the water,   (Swing pole into water)
And hope with all my might,
A little fish will swim on by.   (Left hand — fingers together)
And take a great big bite.   (Move thumb away from fingers — then snap
                             them back together)

THE BALL

Bounce a ball against a wall.   (Toss ball up to wall)
Bounce it on the ground.   (Bounce ball on ground)
Toss it high in the air,   (Throw ball straight up)
And catch it when it comes down.   (Hands together catching ball)

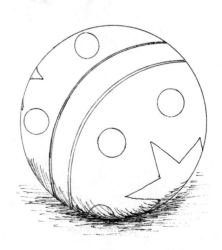

PEEK-A-BOO

Peek-A-Boo, I see you. But you can't see me.
I'm hiding behind my fingers, and not behind a tree.   (Hands in front of eyes, fingers
spread apart to peek through)

If you should try to find me,
And I see you're in sight.
I'll just close my fingers,
And keep them shut up tight.

I'M HIDING

*(Children could do this as a whole group hiding around the room or
the teacher could pick one or two to hide while she reads poem and
children jump up and shout, "Here I am" at the end.)*

I'm Hiding, I'm Hiding.
No one will find me here.
I'll be as quiet as I can be,
When anyone gets near.
And when they've looked all over,
Around and all about.
I'll jump out from my hiding place,
And give a great big shout, "Here I Am!!"

THINGS I CAN DO

I can do a trick like a funny clown.   (Somersault or hop)
I can be stiff like a robot when I walk around.   (Stiff arms and legs)
I can jump and wave pom poms like cheerleaders do.   (Jump, extend arms)
And I can skip rope when I play with you.   (Skip rope)

home

MY WHOLE FAMILY

This is the mother good and dear (Thumb)
This is the father standing near (Pointer Finger)
This is the boy who plays with a ball (Middle Finger)
This is the girl who plays with her doll (Ring Finger)
This is the baby, the pet of all (Little Finger)
See the whole family, big and small! (Show all five fingers)

THIS IS MY FAMILY

This is my mother (Thumb)
This is my father (Pointer Finger)
This is my brother tall (Middle Finger)
This is my sister (Ring Finger)
This is the baby (Little Finger)
Oh, how we love them all. (Clap left hand over all fingers just indicated)

BABY

Here's a ball for baby (Make circle with thumb and pointer)
Big and soft and round.
Here is the baby's hammer. (Make hammer with fist)
Oh, how he can pound!
Here is baby's music. (Hold up hands facing each other)
Clapping, clapping, so. (Clap hands)
Here are baby's soldiers (Hold fingers upright)
Standing in a row.
Here is baby's trumpet. Toot-too, too-too, too.
   (Two fists, one atop the other before mouth)
Here's the way that baby
Plays at peek-a-boo. (Fingers of both hands spread before eyes)
Here's a big umbrella (Bring fingertips together in peak over head)
To keep the baby dry.
Here is baby's cradle. (Make peak of pointers and little fingers and rock)

FUNNY LITTLE MAN

There's a funny little man (thumb) in a funny little house (Wrap fingers around "man")
And right across the way, there's another funny little man in another funny little house.
   (Other hand)
And they play hide and seek all day.
One funny little man through his window peeps (Thumb between fingers)
Sees no one looking, then softly creeps (Thumb crawls out)
Out his door, he comes so slow
Looks up and down and high and low (Thumb up and down)
Then back into his house he goes (Thumb back in fist)
Then the other little man through his window peeps (Thumb between fingers)
Sees no one looking, then softly creeps (Thumb crawls out)
Out his door, he comes so slow
Looks up and down and high and low (Thumb up and down)
Then back into his house he goes (Thumb back in fist)
Sometimes these little men forget to peep
And out of their doors they softly creep (Both thumbs)
Look up and down, high and low
See each other and laugh "Ho ho!"
Then back into their houses they go.

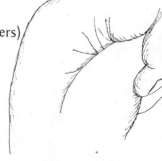

18

A GOOD HOUSE

This is the roof of the house so good   (Make roof with hands)
These are the walls that are made of wood   (Hands straight, palms parallel)
These are the windows that let in the light   (Thumbs and forefingers form window)
This is the door that shuts so tight   (Hands straight side by side)
This is the chimney so straight and tall   (Arms up straight)
Oh!   What a good house for one and all.   (Arms at angle for roof)

DIFFERENT HOMES

A sparrow's home is a nest in a tree,
   (Cup one hand, palm-up; perch other hand on edge)
An octopus's home is a cave beneath the sea.
   (Hook thumbs together; wiggle fingers)
In a hole in the ground a little rabbit hides,
   (Close fingers around thumb; slowly lift thumb, straighten, bend a little)
A sunflower is where a little gnome resides.
   (Palm flat, spread fingers, palm-up; perch other hand in center)
A hollowed-out log is for the porcupine,
   (Place cupped palm palm-down on table; move other fist inside)
But the best home of all is the one that's mine.
   (Point to chest)

MY HOME

When I feel sad   (Wipe away "tear")
Like life's not fair,   (Cross arms across chest)
Or I feel love   (Clasp hands to heart)
I want to share,   (Spread arms wide)
I go to the place   (Walk one hand across other forearm)
Where people love me,   (Point to self)
The place is home
And I'm safe as can be.   (Hug self)

seasons

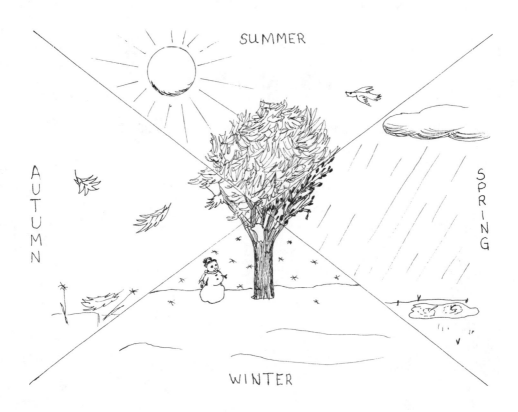

SUMMER

AUTUMN

SPRING

WINTER

AUTUMN

TEN RED APPLES

Ten red apples grow on a tree (Both hands high)
Five for you and five for me (Dangle one hand and then the other)
Let us shake the tree just so (Shake body)
And then red apples will fall below (Hands fall)
1, 2, 3, 4, 5, 6, 7, 8, 9, 10 (Count each finger)

TEN ROSY APPLES

Ten rosy apples high in a tree (Arms above head, fingers separated)
Safely hiding where no one can see.
When the wind comes rocking to and fro. (Arms sway above head)
Ten rosy apples to the ground must go. ("Apples" tumble to the floor)

IN THE APPLE TREE

Away up high in an apple tree (Point up)
Two red apples smiled at me (Form circles with fingers)
I shook that tree as hard as I could (Shake tree)
Down came the apples and m—m—m—m they were good. (Rub stomach)

IF I WERE AN APPLE

If I were an apple
And grew on a tree (Fingertips and thumbs touch overhead to form apple)
I think I'd drop down
On a nice boy like me.
I wouldn't stay there
Giving nobody joy —
I'd fall down at once ("Apple" falls down into lap)
And say, "Eat me, my boy."

AUTUMN

The green leaves are turning,
To yellow, red, and brown.
And when the wind comes whistling by,   (Children make a woo-oo-oo wind sound and
They'll all come sailing down.   twirl around and fall down.)

THE WIND

Feel the strong wind, it almost blows me down,   (Bend body, almost falling)
Hear it whistle through the trees and all around.   (Cup hand to ear)
Try to see the wind as it howls and blows.   (Hands over eyebrows)
But what the wind looks like? Nobody knows!   (Shrug shoulders, palms up)

WHEN THE LEAVES ARE ON THE GROUND

When the leaves are on the ground. (Point to floor)
Instead of on the trees, (Hands clasped over head)
I like to make a great big pile of them
Way up to my knees. (Hands on knees)
I like to run and jump in them (Jump once)
And kick them all around. (Kicking motion with foot)
I like the prickly feel of them
And the crickly, crackly, sound. (Click fingernails)

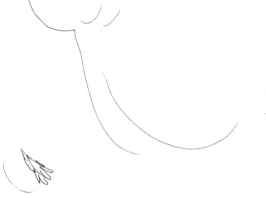

LEAVES

I like to make a pile of leaves,
And jump and tumble around.
I like to hear the dry leaves,
They make such a crunchy sound.

THE CHANGING LEAVES

When autumn comes, the leaves that were green
   (stand with palms up)
Turn yellow and orange and red, I've seen.
   (turn palms over, then point to eye)
Then fall to the ground, and there they die,
   (hands flutter to floor)
'Neath the tree whose branches reach up to the sky.
   (stand with arms upraised)

NOT ALL TREES

Not all trees wear autumn colors. (Shake head)
Some stay green all year. (Hold palms up as if on display)
Their leaves are long (demonstrate) and thin (demonstrate) and sharp,
   (touch index fingertips; jerk one back, "Ouch!")
And at Christmas they bring good cheer. (Touch fingertips above head)

SIGNS OF AUTUMN

When the birds fly south   (Flap arms)
And the wind blows cool   (Shiver)
And the green (hold up hands) on the trees turns red,   (Flip palms over)
And the days grow shorter   (Bring hands close together from far apart)
And the nights grow long   (Separate hands from close together)
And Jack Frost freezes grass dead,   (Point fingers straight up, then slowly curl)
Then summer is gone   (Wave, as if goodbye; rub eye)
And autumn has come   (Turn to opposite direction; hold arms out)
To prepare us for winter's white bed.

FALL

The leaves are green, the nuts are brown,
   (Raise arms sideward, wiggle fingers, make circles for nuts)
They hang so high they would never fall down, (Stretch arms)
Leave them alone till the bright fall weather (Move hands as if wind blows softly)
And then they will all come down together. (Bring arms down to side quickly)

LEAVES ARE FLOATING DOWN

Leaves are floating softly down; (Flutter fingers)
They make a carpet on the ground
Then, swish! The wind comes whirling by (Bring hand around rapidly)
And sends them dancing to the sky. (Flutter fingers upward)

WINTER

BOOTS

Boots never seem to fit. (Hands on hips, shake head)
They're either too big, (Spread arms wide to show size)
And slippy and sloppy.
Or else too small. (Hands together to show size)
And sticky and stucky!
Can't get them off. (Try to pull boots off)
Whether I stand on one leg (Stand on one leg)
Or whether I sit. (Sit down)
Boots never seem to fit! (Hands on hips, shake head)

JACK FROST

Jack Frost is a fairy small, (Show smallness with thumb and pointer)
I'm sure he is out today.
He nipped my nose (Point to nose)
And pinched my toes (Point to toes)
When I went out to play.

BURR-RR-RR

Today I wore my snow suit
That goes from heels to throat. (Point to feet, then neck)
It shuts up with a zip, (Pretend to zip up front)
And is much warmer than a coat.

I wore a sweater under that,
And a wooly cap, bright red. (Make cap on head)
It fitted snug upon my ears (Hands on ears)
And covered my whole head! (Circular motion about head)

I wore overshoes with buckles (Point to shoes)
And mittens lined with fur, (Hand out, fingers together)
I shivered and said, "Burr-rr-rr." (Shiver, arms close to body)

MY ZIPPER SUIT

My zipper suit is bunny brown
The top zips up, (Pretend to zip top up)
The legs zip down. (Pretend to zip leg zippers down)
I wear it every day.
My daddy brought it out from town.
Zip it up, (Pretend to zip top up)
Zip it down, (Pretend to zip leg zippers down)
And hurry out to play.

SNOWFLAKES

Said the first little snowflake (Hold pointer finger up)
As he whirled from the sky,
"I'll light on the red chimney.
It looks nice and high."

Said the second little snowflake, (Hold middle finger up)
"Oh, that is not for me.
I shall feel much safer
In the old apple tree."

Said the third little snowflake. (Hold ring finger up)
"Through the air I'll skim
'Til I light on some boy's shoulder.
Then I'll go to school with him."

MERRY LITTLE SNOWFLAKES

Merry little snowflakes falling through the air;
   (Fingers raised high and moving rapidly)
Resting on the steeple and the tall trees everywhere;
   (Make steeple with two pointer fingers and then raise arms for branches)
Covering roofs and fences, capping every post;
   (Two hands forming roof, then hands clasped)
Covering the hillside where we like to coast.
   (Make scooping motion like coasting)
Merry little snowflakes do their very best
   (Fingers raised high and moving rapidly)
To make a soft, white blanket so buds and flowers may rest;
   (Palms together at side of face)
But when the bright spring sunshine says it's come to stay,
   (Make circle of arms for sun)
Then those little snowflakes quickly run away! (Hide hands behind back)

GATHER SNOW

Gather snow and make a ball. (Hands in ball formation)
Make a snowman round and tall (Indicate with hands)
Coal for buttons. (Pretend to place buttons)
Coal for eyes (Pretend to place eyes)
There he stands and looks so wise, (Stand like a snowman)

MAKE A SNOWMAN

Start with a very tiny ball. (Form ball with fingers)
Roll it through the snow. (Push with right hand)
Over and over and over again. (Repeat pushing motion)
Each turn makes it grow.

Now the ball is big and round (Make ball with arms)
Make it broad and tall. (Indicate with arms)
Add a head and then some arms (Motion as if setting them on)
Firm so they won't fall.

Here are buttons for his coat (Pretend to place)
A broom for him to hold. (Pretend to hold a broom)
Let's put a hat upon his head, (Pretend to put hat on own head)
So he won't get cold.

CHUBBY LITTLE SNOWMAN

A chubby little snowman
Had a carrot nose. (Point to nose)
Along came a bunny
And what do you suppose? (Hold up two fingers on right hand to make a bunny)

That hungry little bunny
Looking for his lunch
Ate that little snowman's nose (Pretend to grab nose)
Nibble, nibble, crunch.

27

LITTLE SNOWMAN

I made a little snowman with hat and cane complete.
   (Hold out hand to indicate little snowman)
With shiny buttons on his coat and shoes upon his feet.
   (Indicate buttons and shoes)
But I know when the sun comes out, my snowman will go away.
   (Make circle with arms)
So I'll put him in our big deep freeze, and he'll be sure to stay.

I AM A SNOWMAN

Now I am a snowman (Stand with arms out)
Standing on the lawn.
I melt and melt and melt
And pretty soon I'm gone.
   (Body slumps and voice fades)

MR. SNOWMAN

(Hold up both thumbs. Wiggle one when the snowman talks and one when the child talks.)

Hello, Mr. Snowman. How are you today? (Wiggle right thumb)
I'm fine little friend. My it's a sunny day! (Wiggle left thumb)
Come on, Mr. Snowman. Come and play with me. (Wiggle right thumb)
But the snowman had disappeared. A puddle was he! (Put left thumb under left hand)

ONCE THERE WAS A SNOWMAN

Once there was a snowman (Stand like a snowman)
Who stood outside my door.
He thought he'd like to come inside
And run around the floor. (Run in small circle)
He thought he'd like to warm himself (Hold hands out before imaginary fire)
By the fireside red.
He thought he'd like to climb upon (Clinging motion)
The big white bed.
So he called to the North Wind
"Help me now, I pray. (Hands together, palm to palm)
I'm completely frozen
Standing here all day." (Huddle arms together)
So the North Wind came along
And blew him in the door
And now there's nothing left of him
But a puddle on the floor. (Point to floor)

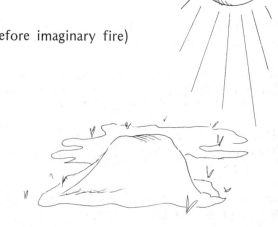

I GODDA CODE

(to be spoken with a stuffed-up nose)

I hab a terrible code id my head.   (Tap nose)
Ah-choo! Ah-choo!   (Sneeze)
So dow I hab to sday id bed.
Ah-choo! Ah-choo!   (Sneeze)
I wed outside widout by coat
Honk! Honk!   (Blow nose)
Ad dow I'be a code ad a lousy sore throat.   (Point to head and throat)
Sniffle, Sniffle.
The dext tibe it raids, pardod by cough,
Cough, cough.
I'll dever take that ode coat off.
Sigh, Siiiiigh.

TREE IN WINTER

Outside the door the bare tree stands   (Palms together high overhead)
And catches snowflakes in its hands,   (Hold above position but open palms
                                          to catch snowflakes)
And holds them well and holds them high
Until a puffing wind comes by.   (Resume first position)

SLEDDING AT HOME

Tune: Mary Had A Little Lamb

Snow piled up will make a hill, make a hill, make a hill.   (Pretend to pile up snow)
Snow piled up will make a hill for sliding in a yard.

We roll it up in great big balls, great big balls, great big balls
We roll it up in great big balls and pound it 'til it's hard.
   (Roll hands and then pound one fist on other palm)

Though other children call to us, call to us, call to us.
Though other children call to us to take our sleds outside.
   (Place hands to mouth)

We don't go out but stay right home, stay right home, stay right home.
We don't go out but stay right home and slide and slide and slide.
   (Make sliding motion with hand)

SPRING

FIVE LITTLE ROBINS

Five little robins up in a tree,
Father (Thumb), Mother (Pointer)
And babies three, (Middle, ring and little fingers)
Father caught a worm, (Point to thumb)
Mother caught a bug, (Pointer finger)
This one got the bug, (Middle finger)
This one got the worm, (Ring finger)
This one said, "Now it's my turn" (Little finger)

FIVE LITTLE SPARROWS

Five little sparrows high in a tree (Hold one hand up)
The first one said, "Whom do I see?" (Point to thumb)
The second one said, "I see the street." (Pointer finger)
The third one said, "And seeds to eat." (Middle finger)
The fourth one said, "The seeds are wheat." (Ring finger)
The fifth one said, "Tweet, tweet, tweet." (Little finger)

TEN LITTLE PIGEONS

Ten little pigeons sat in a line (Hands stretched up over head)
Up on the barn in the warm sunshine.
Ten little pigeons flew down to the ground (Flutter fingers down)
And ate the crumbs that were lying around.

FIVE BABY BIRDS

Five baby birds in a nest in a tree. (Hold up fingers of right hand)
Are just as hungry as they can be.
"Peep", said baby bird number one. (Wiggle little finger)
Mother Bird promised she would come.
"Peep, Peep," said baby bird number two, (Wiggle next finger)
"If she doesn't come, what will we do?
"Peep, peep, peep," said baby bird number three. (Wiggle middle finger)
I hope that she can find this tree.
"Peep, peep, peep, peep," said baby bird number four. (Wiggle next finger)
She never was so late before.
"Peep, peep, peep, peep, peep," said baby bird number five. (Wiggle thumb)
When will our mother bird arrive?
Well, here she comes to feed her family. (Left hand for mother bird)
They're all as happy as they can be.

HOUSES

Here is a nest for the robin; (Cup both hands)
Here is a hive for the bee; (Fists together)
Here is a hole for the bunny; (Finger and thumb form circle)
And here is a house for me! (Fingertips together make roof)

MY PIGEON HOUSE

My pigeon house I open wide (Open fist)
To set my pigeons free (Fingers free)
They fly over fields on every side (Flying)
And then fly back to me. (Fingers return)
And when they return from their merry flight
I close the door, and softly say, "Good-night". (Close fist)

TWO LITTLE BIRDS

High, high, high, up in the sky (Hold both arms up)
The little birds fly (Make fingers fly)
Down, down, down, in the nest (Bring arms down, fingers rest on lap)
With a wing on the left (Hold up left hand)
With a wing on the right (Hold up right hand)
They sleep and they sleep
All through the night.

LITTLE BIRDIE

What does little birdie say
In her nest at peek of day?
"Let me fly," says little birdie, (Wiggle thumb)
"Mother, let me fly away."
Birdie, rest a little longer, (Wiggle other thumb)
'Til your little wings are stronger"
So she rests a little longer.
Then she flies away. (First thumb fly away)

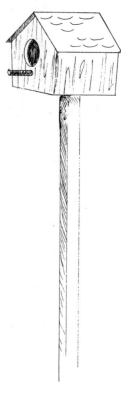

LITTLE BIRDS

Here are two tall telegraph poles (Hold up thumbs)
And between them a wire is strung (Join pointer fingers)
Two little birds are flying by (Wiggle middle fingers)
They hopped on the wire and swang. (Middle fingers on pointers)
To and fro, to and fro (Swing hands back and forth)
They hopped on the wire and swang.

FIVE PRETTY FLOWERS

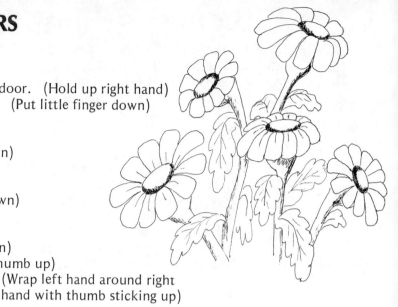

See the five pretty flowers we planted near the door. (Hold up right hand)
A little boy picked one and now there are four. (Put little finger down)
Four pretty flowers for everyone to see,
The dog stepped on one of them,
And now there are three. (Put next finger down)
Three pretty flowers, yellow, pink and blue.
The newsboy threw the paper,
And now there are two. (Put middle finger down)
Two pretty flowers growing in the sun.
A caterpillar chewed the stem,
And now there is one. (Put pointer finger down)
One pretty flower with a smiling face, (Hold thumb up)
I picked the pretty flower and put it in a vase. (Wrap left hand around right
hand with thumb sticking up)

TEN LITTLE LEAF BUDS

Ten little leaf buds growing on a tree (Fingers are buds)
Curled up as tightly as can be (Curl fingers up into fists)
See them keeping snug and warm,
During the winters cold and storm. (Snuggle fist under fist)
Now along comes windy March,
With his breath now soft, now harsh.
First he swings them roughly so (Swing fists back and forth)
Then more gently to and fro (Swing tenderly)
'Til the raindrops from the skies (Stretch arms high, bring down to floor,
tapping fingers as rain)
Falling pitter, patter-wise (Repeat previous action)
Open wide the leaf bud's eyes. (Arms outstretched, open fists and spread
fingers at the word "eyes".)

THE RAINBOW

One day the sun was shining bright. (Hold up right hand for sun)
But clouds came along, it was dark as night. (Hold up left hand for clouds)
The rain began to sprinkle down. (Wiggle both hands for rain coming down)
Soon it was raining all over town.
But when the clouds had passed on by, (Move both hands to the right)
A beautiful rainbow stretched across the sky. (Left hand makes arc over head from
right to left)

SEEDS

I work in my garden,
Plant seeds in a row;
The rain and sunshine   (Flutter fingers, make circle with arms)
Will help them to grow.
Sometimes when the weather
Is too dry and hot,
I sprinkle the earth
With my watering pot.   (Make fist of four fingers, thumb pointing down)
The roots pushing downward,   (Place one hand on the other wrist, fingers on
                                          other hand spread apart and pointing down)
The stems pushing up
My blossoms have opened.   (Hands out, palms up with fingers curling up in
                                          cup-like manner)

LITTLE BROWN SEED

I'm a little brown seed in the ground
Rolled up in a tiny ball;   (Sitting on heels, on the floor, drop head over knees)
I'll wait for the rain and sunshine;   (In the same position, place arms over head
                                          and wiggle fingers downward for rain; then
                                          place both hands in large circle over head,
                                          for sun)
To make me big and tall.   (Stand straight stretching arms over head)

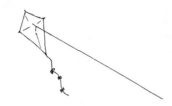
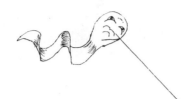
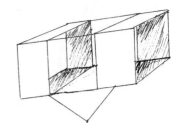

THE KITE

See the kite away up high.   (Use one hand as kite sailing, twisting)
Sailing, swooping in the sky.
Twisting and turning and dipping around,
'Til the wind goes away,
And it comes fluttering down.   (Hand comes slowly down)

STORM

Black clouds are giants hurrying   (Make circle with arms and move quickly)
Across the field of the sky,
And they slip out bolts of lightning
As they go racing by.
When they meet each other
They shake hands and thunder   (Pretend to shake hands)
How do you do!   How do you do!
HOW DO YOU DO!

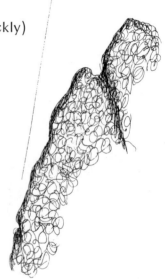

PITTER, PATTER

Oh!   Where do you come from,
You little drops of rain,
Pitter, patter, pitter, patter   (Tap fingers on table or floor)
Down the window pane?

Tell me little raindrops,
Is that the way you play,
Pitter, patter, pitter, patter   (Tap fingers as before)
All the rainy day?

THE GARDEN

(Teacher picks "farmer" / The other children are grouped together. The "farmer" takes children one at a time and places them in a row. Each child crouches down when placed in the row.)
Teacher and children chant together.

See the farmer plant the seeds, plant the seeds, plant the seeds.
See the farmer plant the seeds. He plants them in a row.
Now he has to water them, water them, water them.
Now he has to water them so the seeds will start to grow.
Then the seeds will start to grow, start to grow, start to grow.
Then the seeds will start to grow. Grow up big and tall.
See how big and tall they are, tall they are, tall they are.
See how big and tall they are, standing in a row.
The farmer is so very proud, very proud, very proud.
The farmer is so very proud to see his garden grow.

MY LITTLE GARDEN

In my little garden bed (Extend one hand, palm up)
Raked so nicely over (Use three fingers for rake)
First the tiny seeds I plant
Then with soft earth cover, (Use planting and covering motion)
Shining down, the great round sun (Circle with arms)
Smiles upon it often;
Little raindrops, pattering down, (Flutter fingers)
Help the seeds to soften.
Then the little plant awakes —
Down the roots go creeping, (Fingers downward)
Up it lifts its little head (Fingers held close together pointing upward)
Through the brown earth peeping.
High and higher still it grows. (Raise arms, fingers still cupped)
Through the summer hours,
Till some happy day the buds
Open into flowers. (Spread fingers)

MY GARDEN

This is my garden; (Extend one hand forward, palm up)
I'll rake it with care, (Make raking motion on palm with three fingers of other hand)
And then some flower seeds (Plant motion)
I'll plant in there.
The sun will shine (Make circle with hands)
And the rain will fall, (Let fingers flutter down to lap)
And my garden will blossom (Cup hands together; extend upward slowly)
And grow straight and tall.

35

BUTTERFLY

Bright colored butterfly, (Place hands back to back and wiggle fingers)
Looking for honey,
Spread your wings and fly away,
While it's sunny.

EENSY, WEENSY SPIDER

An eensy, weensy spider (Opposite thumbs and pointer fingers)
Climbed up the water-spout, (Climb up each other)
Down came the rain
And washed the spider out. (Hands sweep down)
Out came the sunshine (Arms form circle overhead)
And dried up all the rain (Arms sweep upward)
And the eensy, weensy spider
Climbed up the spout again. (As above)

FUZZY LITTLE CATERPILLAR

Fuzzy little caterpillar
Crawling, crawling on the ground (Move hand forward, wiggle thumb)
Fuzzy little caterpillar
Nowhere to be found,
Though we've looked and looked
And hunted everywhere around.

HERE IS THE BEE HIVE

Here is the bee-hive. Where are the bees? (Make fist)
They're hiding away so nobody sees,
Soon they'll come creeping out of their hive,
One, two, three, four, five. Buzz-z-z-z-z-z. (Draw fingers out of fist on
                              each count)

THE CATERPILLAR

Crunch, Crunch, went the caterpillar,   (Right hand is caterpillar, left hand is leaf)
"Here's a good leaf to chew".   (Right hand nibbles left hand)
Crunch, crunch. He said, "I'll eat quite a few."
"I'll eat until I'm full and then pretty soon,
I'll spin myself into a snug cocoon."   (Work right hand inside left hand)
(Fold left hand around right hand)

SLEEPY CATERPILLARS

"Let's go to sleep," the little caterpillars said,   (Wiggle fingers)
As they tucked themselves into their beds.   (Make fists)
They will awaken by and by,
And each one will be a lovely butterfly.   (Open hand, one finger at a time)

ROLY-POLY CATERPILLAR

Roly-poly caterpillar
Into a corner crept,
Spun around himself a blanket   (Spin around)
Then for a long time slept.   (Place head on folded hands)
Roly-poly caterpillar
Wakening by and by —   (Stretch)
Found himself with beautiful wings
Changed to a butterfly.   (Flutter arms like wings)

MR. FROG

"Croak, croak," said Mr. Frog as he was sitting in the sun.   (Hold up thumb and wiggle it)
"What a lazy day. Where is everyone?"
"ZZZZ", said the fly as he few up in the sky.   (Left thumb moves by the right thumb)
"I have a hunch Mr. Frog wants me for lunch."
"Buzz, buzz," said the bee, "You won't want me."   (Left hand with pointer finger up for
                                                                            stinger)
"I have a stinger and it's sharp, you see."
"Crick, crick," said the Cricket.   (Left hand, slide thumb against fingers)
"Do you need a friend?"
But Mr. Frog snapped him up and that was the end!   (Right hand grabs left)

GREEN LEAF

Here's a green leaf, (Show hand)
And here's a green leaf, (Show other hand)
That you see, makes two.
Here is a bud (Cup hands together)
That makes a flower;
Watch it bloom for you! (Open cupped hands gradually)

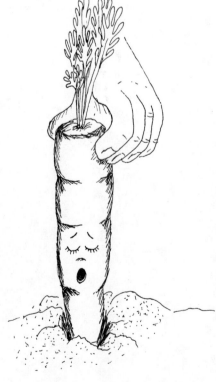

MISTER CARROT

Nice Mister Carrot
Makes curly hair, (Hand on head)
His head grows underneath the ground (Bob head)
His feet up in the air. (Raise feet)
And early in the morning
I find him in his bed (Close eyes, lay head on hands)
And give his feet a great big pull (Stretch legs out)
And out comes his head!

science

MAMMALS

Mammals cover their tender skin
With a layer of fur or hair.
The babies are born, not hatched from eggs,
And when young, need lots of care.
Dogs and cats are mammals that walk
Bats are mammals that fly;
Dolphins and whales are mammals that swim,
And mammals are you and I.

EGGS OR WOMB?

Birds and bees and butterflies (Hook thumb together; flap hands)
All hatch from mother's eggs. (Form egg shape with hands)
Frogs and fish and dragonflies
All hatch from mother's eggs. (Form egg shape with hands)
But cats and cows and kangaroos
All form in mother's womb. (Pat tummy)
And rabbits and rats and reindeer, too,
All form in mother's womb. (Pat tummy)

AMPHIBIANS

An amphibian starts life in a pond
As it hatches from an egg.
It learns to swim with its sturdy tail,
Since it has no arms òr legs.
After a while, as it eats and grows,
Its tail shrinks very small
And its tiny arms and legs grow big
So the amphibian can hop and crawl.

CHICKADEES

Five little chickadees sitting in a door; (Hold up hand)
One flew away and then there were four. (Put down one finger at a time)
Four little chickadees sitting in a tree;
One flew away and then there were three.
Three little chickadees looking at you;
One flew away and then there were two.
Two little chickadees sitting in the sun;
One flew away and then there was one.
One little chickadee sitting all alone;
He flew away and then there were none.

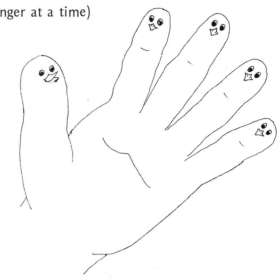

5 LITTLE BIRDS

Five little birds sitting in the sun.
"What can we do for a little fun?"
The first little bird said, "Let's fly around."
The second little bird said, "Let's walk on the ground."
The third little bird said, "I've caught a worm."
The fourth little bird said, "Look at it squirm."
The fifth little bird said, "I want to play."
So he opened his wings and flew away.

BIRDS

The animals that can fly are birds
Because of their wonderful feathers.
They rise with their wings, and steer with their tails,
And frolick alone or together.
Birds build their nests from leaves and twigs
And lay their eggs in batches.
Their parents sit upon the eggs
To warm each till it hatches.

LITTLE BIRD

One little bird with lovely feathers blue (Hold up first finger)
Sat beside another one. Then there were two. (Hold up second finger)
Two little birds singing in the tree.
Another came to join them. Then there were three. (Hold up third finger)
Three little birds, wishing there were more;
Along came another bird. Then there were four. (Hold up fourth finger)
Four little birds, glad to be alive
Found a lonely friend. Then there were five. (Hold up thumb)
Five little birds just as happy as can be
Five little birds singing songs for you and me.

THE KITTEN

I have a little kitten,
Her name is Calico,
I pet her and take care of her,
Because I love her so.

PUSSY CAT

Softly, softly creeps the pussy cat. (Creep fingers on lap)
But the bunny with his two long ears (Hold two fingers in air)
Hops like that!

LITTLE CATS

One little cat and two little cats
Went for a romp one day.
One little cat and two little cats
Make how many cats at play?
Three little cats had lots of fun
Til growing tired, away ran one
I really think he was most unkind to the
Two little cats
That were left behind.

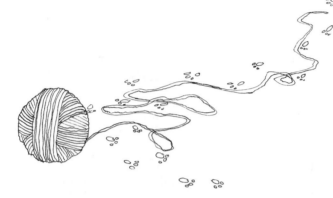

PUSSY

This little pussy drinks her milk,
This little pussy's fur is like silk.
This little pussy wears soiled clothes
This little pussy is Scratch toes!
This little pussy can purr and sing
Oh, she can do most anything.

THIS IS A PUSSY

This is a pussy, sleek and gray (Hold up one thumb)
With her kittens four. (Hold up four fingers)
She went to sleep on the floor (Close eyes)
By the kitchen door.

A KITTEN

A kitten is fast asleep under the chair (Thumbs under hands)
And Donald can't find her.
He's looked everywhere. (Fingers circling eyes to look)
Under the table, (Peek under one hand)
And under the bed. (Peek under other hand)
He looked in the corner and then Donald said,
"Come Kitty, come Kitty, this milk is for you." (Curve hands for dish)
And out came the kitty, calling "Meow, Meow." (Thumbs walk across lap)

IF I WERE A HORSE

If I were a horse, I'd gallop all around. (Slap thigh, gallop in circle)
I'd shake my head and say, "Neigh, Neigh." (Shake head)
I'd prance and gallop all over town.

FIVE LITTLE SQUIRRELS

Five little squirrels sat up in a tree; (Hold up five fingers)
This little squirrel said, "What do I see?" (Point to thumb)
This little squirrel said, "I smell a gun!" (Point to pointer finger)
This little squirrel said, "Oh, let's run!" (Point to middle finger)
This little squirrel said, "Let's hide in the shade!" (Point to ring finger)
This little squirrel said, "I'm not afraid!" (Point to little finger)
Then BANG went the gun! (Clap hands)
And away the little squirrels ran, every one. (Making running motions with fingers)

MY PUPPY

I like to pet my puppy,
He has such nice soft fur.
And if I don't pull his tail,
He won't say Gr-r-r.

MR. OWL

Said Mr. Owl sitting in the tree,
"How would you like to be like me?
"I sleep all day in the bright sunlight,
"And look for my dinner in the middle of the night!"

THIS LITTLE COW

This little cow eats grass; (Hold up one hand, fingers erect, bend down one finger)
This little cow eats hay; (Bend down another finger)
This little cow drinks water, (Bend down another finger)
And this little cow runs away (Bend down another finger)
This little cow does nothing (Bend down last finger)
But lie and sleep all day.

43

TEN LITTLE FROGGIES

Ten little froggies sitting on a lily pad. (All fingers up)
The first one said, "Let's catch a fly." (Teacher's right pinkie down)
The second one said, "Let's go hide." (Teacher's ring finger down)
The third one said, "Let's go for a swim." (Middle finger down)
The fourth one said, "Look I'm in." (Right pointer down)
The fifth one said, "Let's dive." (Right thumb down)
The sixth one said, "There went five!" (Left thumb down)
The seventh one said, "Where did they go?" (Pointer down)
The eighth one said, "Ho, ho." (Middle finger down)
The ninth one said, "I need a friend." (Left ring finger down)
The tenth one said, "This is the end." (Left pinkie down)

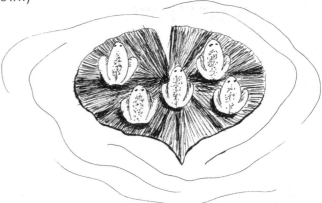

FROGGIES ON A LILY PAD

Five little froggies sitting on a lily pad
The first little froggie said, "Let's try to find Dad."
The second little froggie said, "Oh, let's not, let's not, I'd rather
   swim in a swamp."
The third little froggie said, "Swamps are boring, I'd rather
   catch flies before the rain starts pouring."
The fourth little froggie said, "I'd rather soak in the rain,
   catching flies is such a pain."
The last little froggie said, "Let's get out of this pool and
   go to school."

FISH

A fish has fins which let it swim
In its ocean, lake, or pool.
It has no arms or legs or nose
And groups of fish are a school.
Some fish are fresh-water, some are salt,
All have scales, not hair.
They force some water through their gills
To breathe a little air.

MY FISH

In my room there is a dish (Cup hands)
Full of water and a fish. (Undulate flat palm vertically)
One day its tail gave an extra swish (Make a *strong* undulation)
And now my pet is just a wish. (Palm is horizontal and flat,
                                   slightly curled)

LITTLE TOAD

I am a little toad,
Hopping down the road. (Make fingers hop in time to verses)
Just listen to my song;
I sleep all winter long. (Palms together at side of head)
When spring comes, I peek out (Peek behind hands)
And then I jump about; (Make arms jump)
And now I catch a fly. (Clap hands)
And now I wink my eye (Wink one eye)
And now and then I hop (Make hands hop)
And now and then I stop. (Fold hands)

THIS LITTLE PIG

This little pig went to market, (Point to one finger at a time)
This little pig stayed home,
This little pig had roast beef,
This little pig had none,
This little pig cried "Wee, wee, weee."
And ran all the way home.

EIGHT PIGS

Two mother pigs lived in a pen, (Thumbs)
Each had four babies and that made ten. (Fingers of both hands)
These four babies were black and white. (Fingers of one hand)
These four babies were black as night. (Fingers of the other hand)
All eight babies loved to play. (Wiggle fingers)
And they rolled and they rolled in the mud all day. (Roll hands)

PIGS

Piggie Wig (Thumb) and Piggie Wee (Other thumb)
Hungry pigs as pigs could be
For their dinner had to wait
Down behind the garden gate (Gate made of fingers)
Piggie Wig and Piggie Wee (Wiggle thumbs as named)
Climbed the barnyard gate to see. (Thumbs through fingers)

Peeking through the gate so high
But no dinner could they spy,
Piggie Wig and Piggie Wee got down
Sad as pigs could be,
But the gate soon opened wide
And they scampered forth outside. (Hands swing apart, thumbs run)

Piggie Wig and Piggie Wee,
Greedy pigs as pigs could be
For their dinner ran pell mell
And in the trough both piggies fell. (Make trough with hands, thumbs fall in)

BEES

There is a beehive (Hand cupped)
Where are the bees?
Hidden away where nobody sees.
Now they come creeping out of the hive
One, two, three, four, five. (Extend fingers one by one)
Bzzzzzzzzzzzzzzzzz!

HONEYBEE

Brown and yellow honeybee (Hold up index finger)
Settle on a bloom. (Set index on tip of opposite hand's middle finger)
Sip a little nectar, (Make sipping noises, tap middle finger several times)
Smell the sweet perfume. (Inhale loudly and deeply)
Brown and yellow honeybee (Index finger still on middle finger)
Fly from flower to flower. (Tap other fingertips with index)
Then fly away, for you don't like (Index flies behind back)
The rain of a summer shower. (Drum fingers on table)

SOUNDS OF NATURE

"Buzz, buzz," said the bee as he flew along.
"Tweet, tweet," went the bird as he sang his song.
And the owl in the tree said, "whoo, whoo,"
While down in the barn, the cow said, "Moo."

IF I WERE

If I were a dog,
I'd have four legs to run and play. (Down on all four hands and feet)

If I were a fish,
I'd have fins to swim all day. (Hands at sides making swimming motion)

If I were a bird,
I could spread my wings out wide,
And fly all over the countryside. (Arms out from sides fluttering like wings)

But I'm just little me,
I have two legs, don't you see?
And I'm just as happy as I can be.

THE FARM

The cows on the farm go, moo-oo, moo-oo.
The rooster cries, Cock-a-doodle-doo.
The big brown horse goes, neigh, neigh.
The little lamb says "baa" when he wants to play.
The little chick goes, peep, peep, peep.
The cat says "meow" when she's not asleep.
The pigs say "oink" when they want to eat.
And we say "HELLO" when our friends we meet.

THE BABY MICE

Where are the baby mice?
Hiding in a nest. (Left fist in right hand)
One peeks out. (Left pinkie pops up)
Where are all the rest? (Shrug shoulders)
One is sleepy. (Left ring finger pops up)
One is snappy. (Left middle finger pops up and snap)
One is crying. (Pointer pops up)
And the last one is happy. (Left thumb pops up and wiggles)

5 LITTLE MICE

Five little mice were hungry as could be.
"Let's go to the kitchen and see what we can see."
The first little mouse found a tasty cookie crumb.
He ate it right up and said, "Yum, Yum."
The second little mouse found a piece of jelly bread.
"That snack was pretty good," he said.
The third little mouse said, "For goodness sake,
"Just look at that delicious chocolate cake."
The fourth little mouse found a big piece of cheese.
All of a sudden he started to sneeze.
The fifth little mouse hollered, "We'd better scat.
"Here comes Tommy that big old cat."

THE BUNNY

Once there was a bunny (Fist with two fingers tall)
And a green, green cabbage head (Fist of other hand)
"I think I'll have some breakfast." This little bunny said,
So he nibbled, and he cocked his ears to say,
"I think it's time that I be on my way."

A BUNNY

If I were a bunny,
I'd have ears this tall. (Put hands over head to show how tall)
I could twitch my whiskers, (Use fingers under nose like whiskers)
And wiggle my nose, (Wiggle nose)
But that isn't all ——
I'd be the friskiest bunny,
That you could ever find.
I'd go hippity hop all around,
With my cottontail behind. (Put one hand behind back like a tail and
wave it while hopping around.)

NOT SAY A SINGLE WORD

We'll hop, hop, hop like a bunny (Make hopping motion with hand)
And run, run, run like a dog; (Make running motion with fingers)
We'll walk, walk, walk like an elephant, (Make walking motion with arms)
And jump, jump, jump like a frog, (Make jumping motions with arms)
We'll swim, swim, swim like a goldfish, (Make swimming motion with hand)
And fly, fly, fly like a bird; (Make flying motion with arms)
We'll sit right down and fold our hands, (Fold hands in lap)
And not say a single word!

REPTILES

A reptile breathes like you and me,
Not water, like fish, but air.
Its body is covered with bony plates
Or scales instead of hair.
Some like deserts, some like swamps,
Some like their home a plain.
They hatch from eggs like tiny adults
And in that area remain.

SAMMY

Sammy is a super snake. (Undulate finger on opposite palm)
He sleeps on the shore of a silver lake. (Curl finger to indicate sleep)
He squirms and squiggles to snatch a snack (Undulate finger and pounce)
And snoozes and snores till his hunger is back. (Curl finger on palm)

THE DINOSAURS

The dinosaurs lived long ago
When life on Earth began.
Some were tall, (Stretch hand upwards to show height)
And some were small, (Crouch down low to show height)
Some liked water, (Make swimming motions)
Some land. (Stomp feet)
Pteranodons had leathery wings, (Flap arms)
Brontosaurs, long necks; (Hands on jaw, palms up,
      as if stretching neck upwards)
And the meanest dinosaur of all
Was the Tyrannosaurus Rex! (Feet apart, hands
      clawlike, scowl and growl)

48

WEATHER

The North and South Poles are cold all year round.
Few plants can live on the snow-and-ice ground.

A jungle is wet, hot, and humid all year.
Plants grow and thrive with the animals near.

A forest supports dry land life of all kinds.
From moose to oppossum, from mushrooms to pines.

The prairie is flat, and grasses grow well there.
Few trees survive, but small animals dwell there.

A desert is dry, and few places are hotter.
The life there has learned how to store its own water.

CLIMATOLOGY

Sometimes it gets hot outside
And the sun shines brightly down. (Fan face as if hot)
Sometimes it gets cold outside
And the snow lies white aroun'. (Shiver)
Other times a cloud can fall
And fog comes rolling in. (Wave arms ahead and walk a few
                          paces as if blind)
Or thunder and lightning kick the sky
And make us laugh and grin. (Smile, clap)

THE RAIN

I sit before the window now (Seat yourself, if possible)
And I look out at the rain. (Shade eyes and look around)
It means no play outside today (Shake head, shrug)
So inside I remain. (Rest chin on fist, look sorrowful)

I watch the water dribble down (Follow up-to-down movements with eyes)
And turn the brown grass green. (Sit up, take notice)
And after a while I start to smile
At Nature's washing machine. (Smile, lean back, relax)

DEW AND FROST

On summer mornings, bright and new, (Yawn, stretch)
The grass is wet. We call it dew. (Interlock fingers for grass;
                                    undulate, as if in breeze)
On colder mornings, when breath is white, (Yawn, stretch, shiver)
The dew froze into frost last night. (Interlock fingers stiffly)

THE TERRIBLE TORNADO

One hot summer day (Fan face)
While we played with our ball, (Throw and catch imaginary ball)
The Terrible Tornado (Wear crazy, evil expression, put arms out to
    indicate size)
Came to call. (Continue last action, knock on imaginary door)

We hid far away
From window and door, (Point to each, shake head; crouch down,
    cover head)
While the Terrible Tornado (Rise, wear crazy evil expression again)
Blew wind and roared. (Pucker lips, inflate cheeks, cup hands
    around mouth and *blow*)

He made it rain (Drum fingers on table)
And the trees would sway; (Arms up as if tree, sway in wind)
But soon he grew tired (Yawn, stretch)
And went away. (Slowly, sleepily, collapse to crouch; cover face)

When there was no sound, (Still crouching, raise head)
No peep at all, (Cup hand to ear, look around)
We went outside (Rise, pick up "ball")
And played with our ball. (Throw and catch imaginary ball, as before)

FIRE, EARTH, WATER, AND AIR

Fire will warm us and cook with its heat. (Hold palms out as if warming by fire)
We grow in Earth's soil the plants we will eat. (Crouch and pat ground)
Drinking water is healthy, (Drink from invisible glass)
And last but not least,
People breathe air like all plants and all beasts. (Thump chest, inhale deeply)

THE WIND

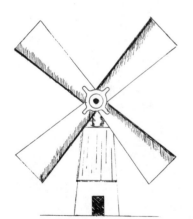

Listen to the wind. (Cup hand to ear)
Hear it blow? (Make "whoosh" noise)
What makes the wind blow?
Do you know? (Point at child)
Fill a balloon up
Full of air. (Cup one hand to lips, blow; with each breath separate
    other hand further from mouth)
Let the air out and (Bring cupped hand away from mouth)
Wind is there. (Bring other hand in front of cupped hand, as if
    feeling breeze)

THE WIND

The wind is a friend when it's at rest, (Clasp hands over stomach)
But sometimes we find the wind is a pest. (Shake head)
When the air is hot, wind cools me off, (Fan face, smile)
But when it's cold, it makes me cough. (Cough)
It turns windmills to give us power, (Make circular motion with arm)
But makes a storm of a summer shower. (Drum fingers on desk, make thunder noises)
It pushes our sailboats and kites and things, (Blow at moving cupped hand)
But also throws sand at us, which stings. (Grasp arm as if hurt)

THE FIVE SENSES

(Writer's note: The teacher may find this series of finger frolicks easier to execute with examples of each poem: either pictures or models of the objects mentioned, or the objects themselves. For that reason, no gestures are included.)

SIGHT

Sight is my most useful sense.
For me, it's number one.
With colors and shapes and sizes and all,
Seeing things is fun!

I can see the blueness of the sky
And the smile on Mama's face.
A photograph of flying birds
And the winner of a race.

I watch where I walk to avoid broken glass
And sharp rocks that will hurt.
I see a rabbit nibbling grass
And the color of my shirt.

HEARING

Sometimes I sit and close my eyes
To find what I can hear.
A jumbo jet sounds far away,
And a barking dog sounds near.

I hear the sound of clapping hands
And the noise of stomping feet.
The scrape of a chair against the floor
As I shift within my seat.

I remember the shout of Santa's laugh,
And the purring of a cat;
The sound of the car as Dad starts it up,
And the buzzing of a gnat.

TOUCH

I can feel all over my skin
In lots of different ways.
I can feel the cold snow on my cheek
And the warmth of the noon sun's rays.

I can feel the roughness of a rock
And the strength of a piece of leather;
The softness of a rabbit fur,
And the lightness of a feather.

I can feel the goosh of modeling clay
As I squeeze it in my hand.
I feel the hardness of the floor,
And the graininess of sand.

SMELL

(Writer's note: Scratch-n-sniffs will suffice if the real items aren't available [like the ocean!]. Equal portions of thyme, rosemary, and oregano in a plastic bag can represent the spices-shelf.)

TASTE

I like the tart taste of a navel orange
As I eat it piece-by-piece;
Bunches of cherries are sweet on my tongue
And I like bacon fried in grease.

I like the mix of sticky tastes
In peanut butter and jelly.
Spaghetti is spicy and sloppy to eat
And it drips onto my belly.

I like Christmas chicken a lot,
And I gnaw it to the bone.
A cold glass of water tastes good with a meal,
As a cold, sweet ice cream cone.

I like the smell of strawberry pie
And roses in the spring;
The scent of a vanilla candle and
Thanksgiving turkey wing.

I like the smell of new-mown grass,
And raked-up leaves in fall.
I like to sniff mom's spice-shelf
And a brand-new basketball.

I like the smell of a sandy beach,
And the salty spray of oceans;
I like the smell of ancient books,
And mama's baby lotion.

SPACE

PLANET EARTH

Our moon Luna is a big round rock
    (Hold up right fist)
And around the earth it runs.
    (Rotate right fist around stationary left)
Planet Earth is a blue-green ball
    (Continue rotating right, shake left for emphasis)
That circles around the sun.
    (Continue rotating right, *and* rotate left around stationary sphere)

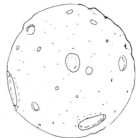

LUNA

As Earth's moon travels on its way ("Orbit" one fist around the other)
It's seen by night (feign sleep) as well as day. (Wake up)
The first day it's skinny, (Hands parallel, close together)
    fourteenth it's round; (Form circle with hands)
Two weeks later it can't be found. (Search heavens, shade eyes)

THE FALLING STAR

I looked up at the dark night sky (Look up, shade eyes)
And saw a falling star pass by. (Smile, point, allow arm to descend)
It died before it hit the ground
And to this day it can't be found. (Inspect floor as if searching)

STARS

The tiny stars you see at night
    (Point upward, count stars)
Are like our sun, so warm and bright,
    (Shade eyes)
But far away, they look so small
    (Separate thumb and index finger by small amount)
They barely give us light at all.
    (Open eyes widely, strain to see)

THE SOLAR SYSTEM

Ten planets make our solar system. (Display ten fingers)
I'll call them off in case you missed 'em. (Display two fists)

The planet closest to our sun
Is Mercury. It's number one. (Raise right pinkie)

The evening star, perhaps you knew,
Is Venus, and our number two. (Raise right ring finger)

The blue-green planet that gave you birth
Is number three; our planet Earth. (Raise right middle finger)

Four is brighter than the stars.
We call this crimson planet Mars. (Raise right index finger)

Jupiter, with its great red spot
Is the largest planet, we are taught. (Raise right thumb)

The colored rings form a pretty pattern
Around the planet we call Saturn. (Raise left thumb)

The seventh planet is not too famous.
It's the one we call Uranus. (Raise left index)

Neptune's next, at any rate,
So we call it number eight. (Raise left middle finger)

The planet Pluto's next in line,
So we give it number nine. (Raise left ring finger)

Persephone was named by men
To be our planet number ten. (Raise left pinkie)

These are the planets, one through ten.
Can you repeat them over again?

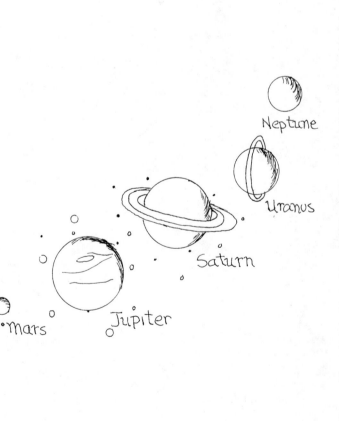

Neptune

Uranus

Saturn

Jupiter

Mars

Earth

Venus

Mercury

Sun

A BIT O' BOTANY

(The Study of Plants)

It's fun to climb the trees outside,
    (Hand-over-hand climbing motion with arms)
They stand so tall and strong.
    (Raise arms to indicate branches)
The lawn of grass hides anthills well,
    (Extend fingers of one hand for grass, "climb" with index
    and middle of other)
Each blade so green and long.

Vines that look like leafy ropes
Up the tree trunks crawl.
    (One forearm becomes vertical for trunk, other arm's index
    and middle fingers "crawl" up)
Bushes look like little trees
    (One forearm is horizontal for ground, other forearm is
    vertical and elbow touches horizontal forearm to make tree)
Without a trunk at all.
    (Lower vertical forearm until only "branches" (hand) touch
    "ground")

PLANTING A BEAN

Here I have a little bean (Hold up tightly curled index finger)
I'm going to plant outside.
I put beans and tools into my wagon (Make appropriate gestures)
And take them for a ride. (Bend over to pick up "wagon" handle;
                        pull and walk)

When I find the perfect spot (Hands on hips, look down, smile, nod)
I get my little rake. (Left hand holds stiff right forearm; right hand
                    is a claw)
I drag it through the surface dirt (Make raking motions)
With care, so it won't break.

Next, I take the shovel out (Right hand claw changes into cup)
And dig a little hole. (Dig)
I drop in the seed and cover it up (Do so; pat surface with back of
                            cupped hand)
And mark it with a pole. (Hammer left hand with right)

Last of all, I water the ground
So the bean is sure to sprout; (Water ground motions)
And the next time I go passing by
A tiny green leaf peeks out. (Hands flatly together on one side; lower
                            index finger pokes up between upper hand's
                            fingers)

THE FOUR FOOD GROUPS

BREAD AND CEREALS

Breads and cereals start from seeds
Of grasses farmers grow;
They're all ground up and mixed with eggs
And other flavors for dough.

The crust of pies and dinner rolls,
And noodles of chicken soup,
Doughnuts, spaghetti, and Cream of Wheat
Are in the bread and cereals group.

DAIRY PRODUCTS

Dairy products are food from the farm
That came from pasture and coop;
Milk from cows and eggs from hens
Are part of the dairy group.

We eat our eggs cooked soft or hard,
Scrambled, poached, or steamed;
From milk we make our cottage cheese,
Our yogurt, and ice cream.

VEGETABLES AND FRUITS

The food we like to eat that grows
On vines and bushes and trees
Are vegetables and fruits, my friend,
Like cherries, grapes, and peas.

Apples and oranges and peaches are fruits,
And so are tangerines.
Lettuce and carrots are vegetables,
Like squash and lima beans.

MEAT, POULTRY, AND SEAFOOD

Cows and pigs and sheep make up
The mammals that we eat.
Spare ribs, steak, or hamburgers,
We call this cooked food "meat".

"Poultry" refers to birds we eat,
Like chicken, duck, and turkey.
"Seafood" is fish and other things
That swim in water murky.

holidays

HALLOWEEN

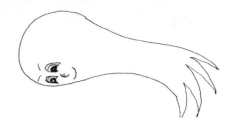

FIVE LITTLE GHOSTS

Five little ghosts dressed all in white
Were scaring each other on Halloween night.
"Boo!" said the first one, "I'll catch you!" (Hold up pointer)
"Wooo" said the second, "I don't care if you do!" (Hold up middle finger)
The third ghost said, "You can't run away from me." (Hold up ring finger)
And the fourth one said, "I'll scare everyone I see." (Hold up little finger)
Then the last one said, "It's time to disappear." (Hold up thumb)
See you at Halloween time next year!"

A FUNNY FACE

I've made a funny false face
With nose and mouth and eyes (Point to nose, mouth and eyes)
And when you see me wear it
You'll have a great surprise (Bring palms of hand together slowly
                                        in gesture of surprise)
For I shall put it on me (Lay hand on either cheek)
And look right straight at you
And in my loudest voice, I'll say (Open eyes wide)
"Boo! hoo! hoo! hoo! hoo! hoo!

ON HALLOWEEN

On Halloween, just take a peek
Wee brownies creep when we are asleep.
Elves and pixies dance and leap.
Witches ride upon a broom.
And fuzzy bats dart past me —— zoom!

CUT INTO A PUMPKIN

Cut into a pumpkin, (Make motion as if cutting with forefinger)
Scoop it with a spoon. (Make scooping motion)
Carve a little mouth that turns
Endwise like a moon. (Form a half circle with thumb and forefinger)
Cut two eyes to twinkle (Make two circles with thumbs and forefingers)
And a big three-cornered nose. (Put forefingers and thumbs together to
form a triangle)

Use for teeth ten shiny seeds
Place in grinning rows. (Hold up ten fingers in a row)
Light a little candle;
And when the shadows fall (Hold up forefinger of left hand for a candle.
Pretend to light)

Set the jolly fellow
In the darkest hall. (Pretend to set pumpkin on shelf)
Listen for the laughter
As folks spy him, (Put one hand behind ear)
Grinning down at all of us

HALLOWEEN SURPRISE

(Tune: Sing A Song Of Sixpense)

First you take a pumpkin (Arms for large pumpkin before stomach)
Big and round and fat
Then you cut the top off (Pretend to slice)
That will make the hat (Hand on head)
Then you hollow out the
Nose and mouth and eyes. (Point to nose, mouth and eyes)
Show it to the children for (Resume first position)
Halloween surprise!

MIXING COLORS FOR HALLOWEEN

First I get my black crayon out
And draw a witch and broom,
A pumpkin and a dark black cat
And a full, bright yellow moon.

Next I mix the yellow and blue
And come up with a green;
The most perfect color for a witch's face
That I have ever seen.

Next I mix the yellow and red
And orange is what I get.
It's the color of my pumpkin's head,
But I'm not finished yet.

Lastly, I mix red and blue
And color the witch's dress
A lovely shade of purple-gray
And then clean up my mess.

59

WIDE-EYED OWL

Here's a wide-eyed owl. (Bring pointer finger and thumb of both hands
together and place before eyes)
With a pointed nose (Make a peak with two forefingers and place before nose)
And claws for toes. (Hands arched before chest fingers curled)
He lives high in a tree (Hands clasped high above head)
When he looks at you (Index finger and thumb of both hands together before
eyes)
He flaps his wings (Bend elbows, flap hands)
And says, "Whoo, whoo-o-o". (Make "whoo" sound)

OWL

An owl sat on the branch of a tree (Owl is right forefinger. The branch is left)
And he was quiet as quiet could be.
'Twas night and his eyes were open like this (Circle eyes with thumb and
forefinger)
And he looked all around; not a thing did he miss (Look about)
Some brownies climbed up the trunk of the tree (Put owl back on perch)
And sat on a branch as quiet as he. (Move middle, ring and little fingers of
right hand next to owl)
Said the wise old owl, "To-Whoo, To-Whoo."
Up jumped the brownies and away they all flew (Make brownies back away
from perch leaving only the
owl sitting on his perch)

PUMPKIN TIME

October time is pumpkin time (Clasp hands before stomach like pumpkin)
The nicest time of year
When all the pumpkins light their eyes (Point to eyes)
And grin from ear to ear. (Point to each ear)
Because they know at Halloween
They'll have lots of fun
Peeking through the window panes (Peek about)
And watching people run. (Make fingers run)

I AM JOLLY JACK-O-LANTERN

Ho! Ho! Little folks (Stand or sit with hands on hips)
Do not be afraid.
I am jolly jack-o-lantern
Out of a pumpkin made.
When I was a pumpkin fat, (Clasp hands before stomach in large
pumpkin formation)
Out in the fields I lay, (Swing pumpkin out to left)
Until a little laddie came
And carried me away. (Move pumpkin slowly to right)
He cut a slit for each eye (Point to eyes)
And another for a nose (Point to nose)
Then carved a great big grinning mouth (Hold right forefinger before mouth
With teeth in funny rows.
He put a candle in my head (Place candle on top of head)
And let the light stream through,
And said, "Oh, Jack-o-lantern, (Hold hand on hips)
Won't I have fun with you!"

60

FIVE LITTLE JACK-O-LANTERNS

Five little Jack-o-lanterns (One hand up)
Sitting on a gate.
The first one said (Point to thumb)
"My, it's getting late."
The second one said, (Pointer finger)
"I hear a noise."
The third one said, (Middle finger)
"It's just a lot of boys."
The fourth one said, (Ring finger)
"Come on, let's run"
The fifth one said (Little finger)
"It's just Halloween fun."
"Puff" went the wind
And out went the light (Close fingers into fist)
And away went the Jack-o-lanterns (Open hand, fingers run behind back)
Halloween night.

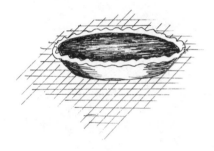

THIS LITTLE PUMPKIN

This little pumpkin was taken to market (Pointer)
And sold for fifteen cents.
This little pumpkin was made into a jack-o-lantern (Middle finger)
And stood high on a fence.
This little pumpkin was made into a pie (Ring finger)
And nevermore was seen
This little pumpkin was taken away (Little finger)
On the night of Halloween.

ONCE THERE WAS A PUMPKIN

Once there was a pumpkin
And it grew (Join the fingers of each hand to make one pumpkin)
And grew (Separate the hand keeping pumpkin formation)
And grew (Join hands before you, making large pumpkin with arms)
Now it's a jack-o-lantern
And smiles at you (Swing pumpkin to left)
And you (Move pumpkin before stomach)
And you (Swing pumpkin to the right)

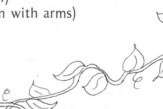

WHAT MAKES YOU RUN?

"What makes you run, my little man,
You are all out of breath?"
A pumpkin made a face at me
And scared me almost to death.

I AM A PUMPKIN

I am a pumpkin big and round.
Once upon a time I grew on the ground.
But now I have a mouth, two eyes, and nos
What are they for do you suppose?
When I have a candle inside, shining bright,
I'll be a jack-o-lantern on Halloween night.

WE HAVE A PUMPKIN

We have a pumpkin, a big orange pumpkin,
We have him two eyes to see where he goes.
We gave him a mouth. We gave him a nose.
We put a candle in. Oh, see how he glows.

61

THANKSGIVING

FIVE LITTLE TURKEYS

Five little turkeys flew up in a tree (One hand up)
The first one said, "There's a man I see." (Point to thumb)
The second one said, "He's coming this way." (Pointer finger)
The third one said, "It's Thanksgiving Day" (Middle finger)
The fourth one said, "What's he going to do?" (Ring finger)
The fifth one said, "He's coming after you." (Little finger)
Chop went the axe before they flew away. (Clap hands on chop)
They all were on the table on Thanksgiving Day. (Make table of one hand
for "turkeys" of other
hand to sit)

FIVE FAT TURKEYS

Five fat turkeys were sitting on a fence. (One hand up)
The first one said, "I'm so immense." (Point to thumb)
The second one said, "I can gobble at you." (Pointer finger)
The third one said, "I can gobble too." (Middle finger)
The fourth one said, "I can spread my tail." (Ring finger)
The fifth one said, "Don't catch it on a nail." (Little finger)
A farmer came along and stopped to say (Pointer finger of other hand)
"Turkeys look best on Thanksgiving Day"

MR. DUCK

Mr. Duck went out to walk (Pointer finger)
In (Snowy, blowy, bright sunshiny, very rainy, dark and cloudy) weather.
He met Mr. Turkey on the way. (Add middle finger)
They stopped and talked together.
Gobble! Gobble! Gobble! Quack! Quack! Quack! (Turkey and duck bob up and
Gobble! Gobble! Gobble! Quack! Quack! Quack! down)
And then they both went back. (Both fingers walk away)

TO GRANDMA'S HOUSE

(Tune: The Farmer In The Dell)

To Grandma's house we go (Make two fists and move them up and down as riding)
Heigh ho, heigh ho, heigh ho.
We're on our way with horse and sleigh
Through fluffy drifts of snow.
Oh, what a trip to take!
She'll have a chocolate cake
There'll be some pies (Hands clasped before stomach)
Of monstrous size
And chestnuts we can bake.
To Grandma's house we go,
Heigh ho, heigh ho, heigh ho.
What lovely things Thanksgiving brings
The nicest things we know.

TABLE STRETCHES

Every day when we eat our dinner,
Our table is very small. (Show size with hands)
There's room for daddy, (Hold up tall finger)
And mother, (Hold up pointer finger)
And baby, that is all, (Hold up little finger)
But when Thanksgiving Day comes
You can't believe your eyes.
For that table stretches (Stretch arms)
Until it is this size!

THE NEW LAND

The Pilgrims sailed the stormy sea
    (Wave hand like water)
To start a country new and free.
They met other people already there,
    (Index and middle fingers of left
    hand "meet" index and middle fingers
    of right)
And they had a great party on the land they would share.
    (Spread arms wide)

THE INDIAN

This is how the Indian brave paddles his canoe,
Splash, splash, splash, splash. (Hands holding a paddle, two strokes
                                     on the right side, two strokes on
                                     the left side)
See how he hunts with his bow and arrow, too.
Zip, zip, zip, zip. (Action of shooting a bow and arrow)

Hear how he beats upon his drum.
Boom, boom, boom, boom. (Action of holding a drum in the left
                                     hand and beating with the right hand)

This is how he dances when day is done.
Woo, woo, woo, woo.
Woo, woo, woo, woo. (Hopping twice on right foot and twice on
                                   the left foot, moving head up and down
                                   while tapping mouth to make the Indian
                                   sound)

THE FIRST THANKSGIVING

When the pilgrims came to this new land,
     (Back of left hand is stationary; two fingers of other hand walk
       toward it)
They met the natives and shook their hand. (Clasp hands; shake)
They had a feast with turkey and corn, (Pretend to eat corn cob)
And that was when Thanksgiving was born.

WAKE UP, LITTLE PILGRIM

Wake up, little pilgrims,
The sun's in the east. (Children sit tall)
Today is the day for our Thanksgiving feast. (Fold hands)
Come, jump out of bed,
See how tall you can stand. (Hold up ten fingers)
My, my but you are a wide awake band!
Wash your hands, wash your faces, (Motion of washing)
So that you will look neat. (Fold hands in lap)
Then come to the table; say prayers before you eat. (Fold hands in prayer)

THE INDIAN

This is how the Indian brave paddles his canoe,
Splash, splash, splash, splash. (Hands holding a paddle, two strokes
                                       on the right side, two strokes on
                                       the left side)

See how he hunts with his bow and arrow, too.
Zip, zip, zip, zip. (Action of shooting a bow and arrow)

Hear how he beats upon his drum.
Boom, boom, boom, boom. (Action of holding a drum in the left
                               hand and beating with the right hand)

This is how he dances when day is done.
Woo, woo, woo, woo.
Woo, woo, woo, woo. (Hopping twice on right foot and twice on
                          the left foot, moving head up and down
                          while tapping mouth to make the Indian
                          sound)

THE FIRST THANKSGIVING

When the pilgrims came to this new land,
     (Back of left hand is stationary; two fingers of other hand walk
     toward it)
They met the natives and shook their hand. (Clasp hands; shake)
They had a feast with turkey and corn, (Pretend to eat corn cob)
And that was when Thanksgiving was born.

WAKE UP, LITTLE PILGRIM

Wake up, little pilgrims,
The sun's in the east. (Children sit tall)
Today is the day for our Thanksgiving feast. (Fold hands)
Come, jump out of bed,
See how tall you can stand. (Hold up ten fingers)
My, my but you are a wide awake band!
Wash your hands, wash your faces, (Motion of washing)
So that you will look neat. (Fold hands in lap)
Then come to the table; say prayers before you eat. (Fold hands in prayer)

HANUKKAH

THE CANDLE

ee the candle shine so bright.
urning brightly day and night.
s the lamp did long ago.
ringing the message with its glow.

HANUKKAH

anukkah is the Feast of Lights.
's a time we dedicate.
e light the candles,
nd exchange our gifts.
s Hanukkah we celebrate.

HANUKKAH

lanukkah tells of a struggle.
t happened many years ago.
he little bit of oil in the lamp,
asted eight days, we know.
o we light a candle every day,
Intil eight are burning bright.
o help us all remember
hat very special light.

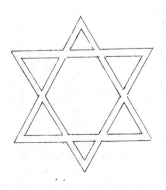

MENORAH

Menorah, Menorah, your candles we will light.
Menorah, Menorah, the flames will shine so bright.
We light one candle every day,
'Til eight are burning,
In a grand display.
These candles we dedicate,
As Hanukkah we celebrate.

65

CHRISTMAS

A RIDE FROM SANTA

If I could find old Santa, I'd ask him for a ride.
And in the wooly blankets, I'd snuggle by his side.
And when we go up high, to the chimneys tall,
I would stay up on the roof, for fear that I would fall
And when the reindeer start to go.
I'd call out loudly, Whoa! Reindeer! Whoa!

HERE IS A CHIMNEY

Here is a chimney deep and wide. (Raise arms straight up)
Do you think Santa can get inside?
Here is the fireplace warm and black (Forearms horizontal, middle fingers
                                                    touching)
And here is old Santa's bursting pack. (Hand clasped before stomach)
Here are the stockings one — two — three; (Hold fingers up at each count)
Hanging side by side you see.
Here is the book that Santa bought (Hands side by side, palms up)
And here is the kite that Bobby bought. (Arms up fingertips touching)
Here is a ball so soft and round (Fingers touching in ball shape)
And here is a hammer pound, pound, pound. (One fist pounds other)
Here is a music box — clap, clap, clap, (Clap three times)
A bag of candy for each girl and boy (Hold fists out)
Surely their hearts will fill with joy.
Then over the roof and far away,
Dashes old Santa and his sleigh. (Right pointer upright between left
                                          pointer and middle finger dash away)

HERE'S SANTA

Here's Santa, jolly and gay, (Hold up thumb on left hand)
He'll soon be on his way.
Here's Mrs. Santa, making toys (Hold up thumb on right hand)
For all good girls and boys.
Come Dancer, Prancer, Dasher, and Vixon, (Hold up four fingers on left hand;
                                                      point to them)
Come Comet, Cupid, Donner and Blitzen, (Hold up four fingers on right hand;
                                                    point to them)
Now, away to your housetop, (Point to a friend)
Clickety-clop, clickety-clop, clickety-clop. (Clapping motion, loud, soft, softer)

66

FIVE LITTLE BELLS

Five little bells hanging in a row (Hold up hand)
The first one said, "Ring me slow." (Point to thumb)
The second one said, "Ring me fast." (Pointer finger)
The third one said, "Ring me last" (Middle finger)
The fourth one said, "I'm like a chime." (Ring finger)
The fifth one said, "Ring me at Christmas time." (Little finger)

CLAP YOUR HANDS

Oh clap, clap your hands, and sing out, with glee, (Clap)
For Christmas is coming, and merry are we.
Now over the snow came Santa's reindeer
They scamper and scamper to bring Santa here.
We'll hang up our stockings and when we're asleep!
Down into our houses Old Santa will creep.
He'll fill all our stockings with presents and then
Santa Claus and his reindeer will scamper again,
So clap, clap your hands and sing out with glee (Clap)
For Christmas is coming and merry are we.

CHRISTMAS BELL

I'm a little Christmas bell
I like to sing a Christmas song
When I sing,
You hear me ring
Ding dong, ding dong.

EIGHT REINDEER

Eight little reindeer playing in the snow
Eight little reindeer at the North Pole.
All of them anxious for Christmas Day
Waiting for Santa to say, "Up, up and away"

FIVE LITTLE REINDEER

The first little reindeer went to the market to buy some Christmas trees.
The second little reindeer went to the elf shop to supervise the toys.
The third little reindeer hurried to the cookie factory to prepare for girls and boys.
The fourth little reindeer went to the TV stations to ready the Christmas shows.
And the fifth little reindeer went to see Heat Miser and Cold Hiser to order the season's snows.

CHRISTMAS TREE

Here is Bobby's Christmas tree (Stand right hand upright)
Standing right up tall.
Here's a pot to hold its trunk (Cup left hand under right hand)
So that it won't fall.
Here are balls to make it gay (Thumb and pointer fingers in ball formation)
One ball, two balls, see?
And here are two bright lights of red (Right pointer and middle fingers upright)
To trim the Christmas tree.

CHRISTMAS TREE

I'm a Christmas tree (Arms extended slightly)
High or low (Raise up and down)
If I'm on my knee (On knees)
Or on my toe. (Up on toes)

67

ALISA

Alisa was a little elf   (Hold right hand above left to show size)
With tiny pointed ears.   (Point at ear)
She worked for Mister Santa Claus
For For fifty-seven years.

One day he took her by the hand   (Bend over to one side as if taking an
                                              elf's hand)
And said, "Please come with me."
He took her in his living room   (Still bend over, walk to a chair)
And sat her on his knee.   (Sit in chair, pretend to put elf on lap)

"You've been so good and worked so hard,
Here's your reward," he said.   (Waggle finger "at" elf)
"When I go out on Christmas Eve
You'll help me in my sled."

Alisa laughed and clapped her hands   (Laugh, clap)
And cried, "That will be fun!
I'll help you give good kids their toys
Until the job is done!"   (Smack fist against open palm)

So Santa had good help that year
And every year thereafter,
As Alisa passed to girls and boys   (Work hands as if dealing cards)
The gifts of love and laughter.   (Smile; put hands on belly with laughter)

SANTA

When Santa comes down the chimney   (Downward motion with hands)
I should like to peek   (Peek through fingers)
But he'll never come, no never   (Shake head)
Until I'm fast asleep.   (Palms together beside head)

ON A COLD WINTER NIGHT

On a cold winter night   (Shiver)
With no place to stay,   (Still shivering, look around)
A baby was born   (Position arms as if holding infant)
In a manger of hay.   (Cup hands)
He cried for his dinner   (Rub eyes)
And stared at a sheep,   (Open eyes widely)
He smiled at his mother   (Smile widely)
And fell fast asleep.   (Lay cheek on palm, close eyes)
Three wise men came by   (Clasp hands, bow low)
And said, "If he pleases,
We have gifts to give   (Cup hands, hold close to body)
To the infant named Jesus."   (Extend cupped hands to viewer
Their mission then finished
The men hummed along   (Stand with hands behind back)
As a poor little drummer boy
Played Jesus a song.   (Slap thighs)

68

GAY VALENTINES

Five gay valentines (Hold up five fingers)
From the ten cent store
I sent one to Mother, (Bend down a finger)
Now there are four.
Four gay valentines
Pretty ones to see?
I give one to Brother, (Bend down finger)
Now there are three.
Three gay valentines,
Yellow, red and blue?
I give one to Sister, (Bend down finger)
Now there are two.
Two gay valentines.
My, we have fun;
I give one to Daddy, (Bend down finger)
Now there is one.
One gay valentine,
The story is almost done;
I give it to Baby, (Bend down finger)
Now there are none.

VALENTINE'S DAY

I'm glad it's Valentine's Day, today.
It's a special day, you know.
It gives me an extra chance,
To say, "I Love You So".

VALENTINE

I have a Valentine for you.
It's made with ribbon and lace.
I hope when you read, "I Love You",
It will put a smile on your face.

PRETTY VALENTINE

To every little friend of mine,
I'll send a pretty valentine. (Make heart shape with thumbs and pointers)
You'll find a message, if you'll look. (Open palms)
I'll use an envelope for this. (Two fists together)
I'll write my name, then seal a kiss. (One hand closes on fingers of other)
What color shall I give to you?
Orange, purple, green, or blue?
Yellow or pink? White or red?
Or maybe a lacy one instead.

A DAY FOR LOVE

Pretty red hearts (Trace outline of heart in air with index fingers)
And two-by-two. (Hold up two fingers of both hands)
Holding hands (Clasp hands together)
And "I love you." (Clasp hands to heart)
Scented flowers (Hand "holds" flower to nose; sniff)
From garden vines.
A day for love; St. Valentine's.

MOM'S CARD

Today I'll make a pretty card
With paper and a pen. (One flat palm is paper, other index is pen)
I'll fold the paper card in half (Bend fingers inward)
And draw some hearts and then (Draw hearts in air with finger)
I'll draw my face and sign my name
And hide it on her tray, (Put closed fist behind back)
So when she wakes up, she'll see the card (Bring "card" in front, look
                                             surprised)
Say "Happy Valentine's Day!" (Trace finger over "card" as if reading it)

A MAILBOX VALENTINE

When you look in your mailbox,
What do you think you'll see? (Children pretend looking in mailbox)
It might be a Valentine,
And it might be from me. (Children point to themselves)

BUNNY IN THE WOOD

There was a bunny who lived in the woods.
He wiggled his ears as a good bunny should (Forefinger on either side of head
        for ears)
He hopped by a squirrel (Hold two fingers up and close others on one hand
        and take one jump down other arm)
He hopped by a tree (Take another hop)
He hopped by a duck (Take another hop)
And he hopped by me. (Hop over the opposite fist)
He stared at the squirrel,
He stared at the tree,
He stared at the duck,
But he made faces at me. (Wiggle nose)

MAKE A RABBIT

Oh, can you make a rabbit (Pointer and middle fingers up)
With two ears, so very long?
And let him hop, hop, hop about (Rabbit hops)
On legs so small and strong?
He nibbles, nibbles carrots (Insert second finger on left hand for the carrot
        between the thumb, fourth and fifth fingers of
        the right hand representing the mouth. Open and
        close the fingers to imitate nibbling)
For his dinner every day.
As soon as he has had enough
He scampers far away. (Rabbit scampers away)

HOP!

Creeping, creeping, creeping (Walk two fingers down other arm)
Comes a little cat.
But bunny with his long ears (Pointer and middle finger up for ears)
Hops! Like that! (Pointer and middle finger hop down other arm)

BUNNIES

"Come my bunnies, it's time for bed,"
That's what mother bunny said,
"But first I'll count you just to see
If you have all come back to me;
Bunny one, Bunny two, Bunny three, Bunnies so dear
Bunny four, Bunny five, Yes, You're all here.
You're all here.
You're the sweetest things alive
My bunnies, one, two, three, four, five."

EARS SO FUNNY

Here is a bunny with ears so funny (Right fist with two fingers raised)
And here is his home in the ground (Cup left hand)
When a noise he hears, he pricks up his ears,
And jumps to his home in the ground. (Right two fingers dive into cupped
        left hand)

SWEET BUNNY

There is nothing so sweet as a bunny (Hands on head for bunny ears)
A dear, little, sweet, little bunny.
He can hop on his toes (Hop forward)
He can wiggle his nose (Wiggle nose)
And his powder puff tail is quite funny. (Ball formation with hands)

EASTER RABBIT

A rabbit came to my house once,
With funny, stretched-out ears (Hands on head like bunny ears)
His nose was full of wiggles, and (Wiggle nose)
His eyes were full of fears (Point to eyes)
I said, "Why do you twitch your nose?
Is that a bunny habit?
And are you called the 'March Hare'
Or called the 'Easter Rabbit'?"
He never said a word; but bounced (Hands on head like bunny ears)
Away on pushing legs; (Hop forward)
But, oh, he left behind a nest (Look backward over a shoulder)
Of colored Easter eggs!

CABBAGE HEAD

Once there was a rabbit (Pointer and middle fingers up)
And a green cabbage head (Fist of left hand)
"I think I'll have some breakfast."
So he nibbled and he nibbled (Rabbit nibbled cabbage)
And he cocked his head to say,
"I guess this little rabbit
Should hop—hop—hop away." (Rabbit hops away)

CHOCOLATE BUNNY

The sweet chocolate bunny poked out his head (Wrap fingers on left hand around right thumb; have end of thumb peeking out)

Then wiggled his ears (Wiggle second and third finger of right hand)
"It's Easter" he said,
"And good boys and girls are waiting to see
What sweet chocolate bunny (Cup fingers of left hand and pretend to put something in it with right hand)

Will hide in his tree."
The hen said, "Basket of eggs (Interlock fingers of hands to make a basket)
I'll give you."
The honey bee said, "I've paste (Cup fingers of right hand)
for you, too."
The warm shining sun said, (Form a circle with the fingers of both hands)
"And for my good deed
I'll melt all the chocolate
that you're going to need."
So the sweet chocolate bunny (Join right index finger and thumb in gesture of holding a brush)

With his tail for a brush
Painted each egg
With sweet chocolate mush
And then with his whiskers
And honey bee paste
The name of a child (Pretend to write on back of left fist with right hand)
On each egg he traced.

71

COUNTING EGGS

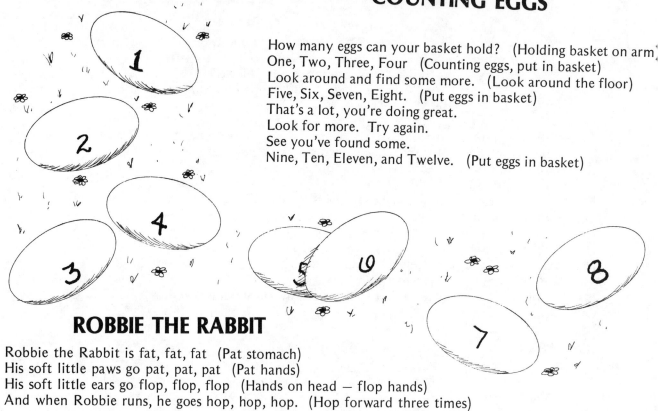

How many eggs can your basket hold?   (Holding basket on arm)
One, Two, Three, Four   (Counting eggs, put in basket)
Look around and find some more.   (Look around the floor)
Five, Six, Seven, Eight.   (Put eggs in basket)
That's a lot, you're doing great.
Look for more. Try again.
See you've found some.
Nine, Ten, Eleven, and Twelve.   (Put eggs in basket)

ROBBIE THE RABBIT

Robbie the Rabbit is fat, fat, fat (Pat stomach)
His soft little paws go pat, pat, pat (Pat hands)
His soft little ears go flop, flop, flop (Hands on head — flop hands)
And when Robbie runs, he goes hop, hop, hop. (Hop forward three times)

MEMORIAL DAY

WAVING THE FLAG

Take the flag and wave it.
Hold it high above,
See its' colors, red, white, and blue,
Our American flag we love.

THE FLAG

*(One child or teacher holds the flag as the children
all follow along in a row.)*

We love our flag,
The red, white, and blue.
We stand at attention,
And salute her, too. (All salute)

We pledge our allegiance, (Hands over heart)
To our country big and strong.
We are tall and straight like soldiers,
As we march along.

72

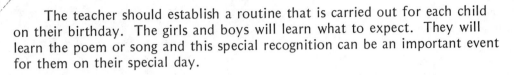

BIRTHDAYS

The teacher should establish a routine that is carried out for each child on their birthday. The girls and boys will learn what to expect. They will learn the poem or song and this special recognition can be an important event for them on their special day.

Perhaps the teacher could use a wall chart with the current month and then the names and dates of the children who have a birthday during that month. Also, pictures of candles could be pasted or drawn next to each child's name according to how old they are going to be.

Have a specially painted or decorated chair for the birthday child to use on their special day. Also, a paper crown, decorated with stars and their name on it could be easily constructed and the child would wear this for the day and take it home.

The birthday child could be the special helper for the day; passing out materials, treats, etc. Also, the birthday child could be the line leader, or select the game to be played or pick a special record or story for the day.

TODAY'S BIRTHDAY

Today is _____'s birthday; (Insert the name of the child)
Let's make her (him) a cake;
Mix and stir, (Action of stirring)
Stir and mix,
Then into the oven to bake. (Pretend to hold the cake in two hands)
Here's our cake so nice and round; (Make a circle with arms)
We frost it pink and white; (Action of spreading frostings)
We put six (any number) candles on it,
To make a birthday light.

MY DAY

One day of the year is a special one. (Point finger up)
If you are a daughter or a son. (Hands out holding skirt, hands in pockets)
Sometimes this day is very quiet or very loud. (Pointer over mouth,
                                          hands over ears)
But because it's our day we're very, very proud. (Thumbs under underarm)
And friends and relatives come over to say. (Fingers on both hands inverted
                                          and do walking motion on lap)
Congratulations to you and Happy Birthday!! (Hands up high)

LOOK AT ME

Please everybody look at me (Point to self)
Today I'm five year's old you see (Hold one hand up)
And after this I won't be four (Hold four fingers up)
Not ever, ever any more!

I won't be three (Three fingers up)
or two (Two fingers)
or one. (One finger)
For that was when I'd first begun.
Now I'll be five for a while, and then (Five fingers up again)
I'll be something else again.

BIRTHDAY CELEBRATION

(Birthday child stands in front)

We have a birthday to celebrate, (Class repeats together)
So put the candles on the cake.
How many candles do you need?

(Birthday child responds with their age)

Count the candles and let's all say,
We wish you a very Happy Birthday. (They all count the candles
and shout, "HAPPY BIRTHDAY")

YOUR SPECIAL DAY

Today is your special day to have the birthday chair.
You will be the leader and have a birthday crown to wear.
So everyone will know this is your special day,
As we celebrate your _____ birthday. (Fill in with proper year.)

the world around us

CIRCUS AND ZOO

CIRCUS CLOWN

I'd like to be a circus clown,
And make a funny face. (Make funny face)
And have all the people laugh at me,
As I jump around the place. (Act silly, make a face)

TEN CIRCUS WAGONS

Ten circus wagons, painted oh so gay,
Came into town with the circus today! (Hold up ten fingers)
This one holds a lion
That gives a big, loud roar! (Point to thumb)
This one holds a tiger
Fast asleep upon the floor. (Pointer finger)
This one holds a funny seal
That nods to left and right. (Middle finger)
This one holds a zebra
That is striped all black and white. (Ring finger)
This one holds a camel
With two humps upon his back. (Little finger)
This one holds a panther
With his coat of fur so black. (Thumb of other hand)
This one holds an elephant
That is drinking from a pail. (Pointer finger)
This one holds a monkey
That is swinging by his tail. (Middle finger)
This one holds a hippo
With a grin so very wide. (Ring finger)
This one holds a leopard
With a gaily spotted hide. (Little finger)
Ten circus wagons, painted oh so gay,
Came into town with the circus today! (Ten fingers)

FIVE LITTLE CLOWNS

Five little clowns walk on stage. (Teacher's right hand fingers pointing
           down walking motion)
This little clown tells his age. (Right pinkie up)
This little clown has a red suit. (Right ring finger up)
This little clown is very cute. (Right middle finger up)
This little clown is very sad. (Right pointer up)
This little clown is glad. (Right thumb up and wiggle)
Five little clowns walk off stage. (Continue left to right motion by moving
           right hand fingers pointing down to
           instructor's left.

THIS LITTLE BEAR

This little bear has a fur suit, (Thumb)
This little bear acts very cute, (Pointer finger)
This little bear is bold and cross, (Middle finger)
This little bear says, "You're not boss." (Ring finger)
This little bear likes bacon and honey; (Little finger)
But he can't buy them, he has no money!

THIS LITTLE TIGER

This little tiger is very wild, (Thumb)
This little tiger is a loving child. (Pointer finger)
This little tiger has some big black spots, (Middle finger)
This little tiger has small black dots; (Ring finger)
This little tiger likes to prowl and smell, (Little finger)
But his teeth are too small to bite very well.

TWO LITTLE MONKEYS

Two little monkeys (Pointer and middle finger up)
Fighting in bed.
One fell out (Middle finger down)
And hurt his head
The other called the doctor (Pointer finger of other hand)
And the doctor said:
"That's what you get
for fighting in bed." (Shake "doctor" finger at "monkeys")

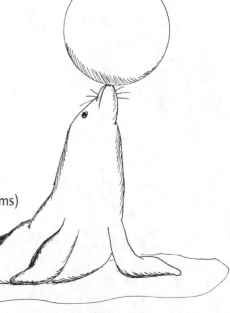

SEALS

The seals all flap their shining flips (Put hands under arms and flap arms)
And bounce balls on their nosey tips, (Point to nose)
And beat a drum and catch a bar, (Beat drum)
And wriggle with how pleased they are. (Wriggle)

FIVE LITTLE POLAR BEARS

Five little polar bears, (Hold up one hand)
Playing on the shore;
One fell in the water
And then there were four. (Put down one finger as you say each verse)

Four little polar bears,
Swimming out to sea;
One got lost,
And then there were three.

Three little polar bears said
"What shall we do?"
One climbed an iceberg
Then there were two.

Two little polar bears
Playing in the sun;
One went for food,
Then there was one.

One little polar bear,
Didn't want to stay;
He said, "I'm lonesome,"
And swam far away.

MONKEY SEE, MONKEY DO

Monkey see, will monkey do?
Let's watch them in the zoo.
We stare in. (Pupils left hand up)
They look out. (Pupils right hand up palms facing each other)
We eat popcorn. (Pupils left hand fingers touching thumb)
They eat fruit. (Pupils right hand fingers sway)
We stand up. (Pupils left hand fingers up straight)
They sit down. (Pupils right hand fingers down)
Monkey see, monkey do?
Not from what we see in the zoo.

THE FUNNY FAT WALRUS

The funny, fat walrus sits in the sea
Where the weather is freezing and cold as can be. (Put hands on arms and shiver)
His whiskers are droopy and his tusks are white,
And he doesn't do much but sit day and night.

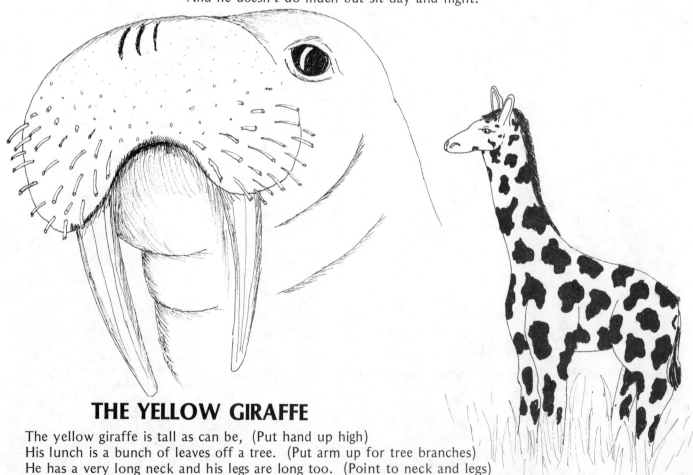

THE YELLOW GIRAFFE

The yellow giraffe is tall as can be, (Put hand up high)
His lunch is a bunch of leaves off a tree. (Put arm up for tree branches)
He has a very long neck and his legs are long too. (Point to neck and legs)
And he can run faster than his friends in the zoo. (Run in place)

FIVE GRAY ELEPHANTS

Five gray elephants marching through a glade (March fingers of right hand)
Decide to stop and play they are having a parade.
The first swings his trunk and announces he'll lead, (Swing arm like trunk)
The next waves a flag which of course they need. (Wave hand over head)
The third gray elephant trumpets a song, (Blow through hand)
The fourth beats a drum as he marches along. (Beat a drum)
While the fifth makes believe he's the whole show
And nods and smiles to the crowd as they go. (Nod head to left and right, smile)
Five gray elephants marching through the glade
Having a lot of fun during their parade.

THE ELEPHANT'S TRUNK

The elephant has a great big trunk (Pretend an arm is the trunk)
That goes swinging, swinging so. (Swing trunk)
He has tiny, tiny eyes that show him where to go. (Point to eyes)
His huge long ears go flapping, flapping up and down, (Pretend hands are ears)
His great feet go stomping, stomping on the ground. (Stomp with feet)

THE KANGAROO

Said the king kangaroo,
"What can I do? (Hold out hands with palms up)
If I had a cradle, I'd rock it. (Cup hands and move back and forth)
But my baby is small
So I think after all,
I'll carry him 'round in my pocket!" (Put one hand on stomach for a pocket
                              and the other inside "pocket")
Jump, jump, jump goes the big kangaroo. (Jumping motion with pointer and
                              middle fingers; other fingers and
                              thumb folded)
I thought there was one, but I see there are two
The mother and a baby, See his head pop out, (Thumb comes between pointer
                              and middle finger)
Of her cozy pocket, while he looks about
Yes, he can see what's going on
As his mother jumps along (Repeat jumping motion with thumb showing)
Jump, jump, jump,
Jump, jump, jump,
Jump, jump, jump.

THE BROWN KANGAROO

The brown kangaroo is very funny
She leaps and runs and hops like a bunny. (Hop)
And on her stomach is a pocket so wide, (Put hand on stomach like a pocket)
Her baby can jump in and go for a ride. (Have other hand jump into "pocket")

COMMUNITY HELPERS

BAKER'S TRUCK

The baker man's truck comes down the street
Filled with everything good to eat;
Two doors the baker man opens wide; (Stretch arms apart)
Now, let us look at the shelves inside.
What do you see? What do you see? (Hands over eyes)
Doughnuts and cookies for you and me; (Make circles with thumbs and pointers)
Cinnamon rolls. (Make larger circles)
And pies, (Make even larger circles)
And bread too;
What will he sell to me and to you?

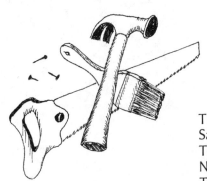

THE CARPENTER

This is the way he saws the wood (Right hand saws left palm)
Sawing, sawing, sawing;
This is the way he nails a nail (Pound right fist on left palm)
Nailing, nailing, nailing;
This is the way he paints the house (Right hand paints left palm)
Painting, painting, painting.

CARPENTER

The carpenter's hammer goes tap, tap, tap, (Pound fists together)
And his saw goes see, saw, see (Right hand saws left arm)
And he planes and he measures (Bend fingers of right hand and slide down
         left arm)
And he hammers and he saws (Hammer and saw as in above)
While he builds a big house for me. (Elbows bent, forearms upright with
         fingertips touching)

HELPING DAD

This is the way I pound a nail,
When I'm busy helping my dad.
And when he sees how hard I work,
He smiles and he is glad.

MY TEACHER

My teacher taught me how to read, (Point to eyes)
And how to sing some songs; (Hand on chest, head back, sing "la la!")
She/He taught me how to tell the time, (Point to wrist)
And how to grow healthy and strong. (Display biceps like strong man)
My teacher taught me how to count (Hold up one, two, three fingers)
And how to tie a knot; (Feign tying shoe)
She/He taught me how to jump a rope — (Jump)
My teacher knows a lot. (Pat temple)

TEN BRAVE FIREMEN

Ten brave firemen sleeping in a row, (Fingers curled to make sleeping men)
Ding, dong, goes the bell, (Pull down on the bell cord)
And down the pole they go. (With fists together make hands slide down pole)
Off on the engine oh, oh, oh. (Pretend a nozzle with fists to use hose)
When all the fire's out, home so-o-slow.
Back to bed, and in a row. (Curl all fingers again for sleeping men)

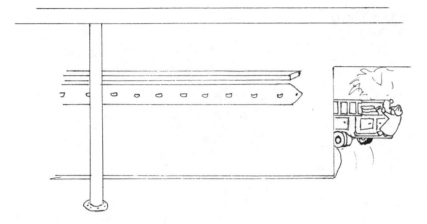

THE FIREMEN

Clang, Clang, goes the fire truck.
When it is racing about.
The firemen will work very hard,
To put the fire out.
With their hoses and their ladders
They answer the fire call.
When the firemen fight the fires,
They really help us all.

MAIL

Five little letters lying on a tray. (Extend fingers of right hand)
Mommy came in and took the first away. (Bend down thumb)
Then Daddy said, "This big one is for me."
I counted them twice now there were three. (Bend down pointer finger)
Brother Bill asked, "Did I get any mail?"
He found one and cried, "A letter from Gale!" (Bend down middle finger)
My sister Jane took the next to the last.
And ran upstairs to open it fast. (Bend down ring finger)
As I can't read, I'm not able to see
Whom the last one's for, but I hope it's for me! (Wiggle the little finger,
                                                                          then clap hands)

MR. POLICEMAN

Mr. Policeman wears a silver badge
On his uniform of blue.
He makes us all obey the law,
And he helps us when we need him, too.

TRAFFIC POLICEMAN

The traffic policeman holds up his hand. (Hold up hand, palm forward)
He blows the whistle, (Pretend to blow whistle)
He gives the command. (Hold up hand again)
When the cars are stopped. (Hold up hand again)
He waves at me.
Then I may cross the street you see. (Wave hand as if indicating for
                                                            someone to go)

SAFETY
THE CROSSING GUARD

The crossing guard keeps us safe as he works from day to day.
He holds the stop sign high in the air,
For the traffic to obey.
And when the cars have completely stopped,
And it's safe as it can be,
He signals us to walk across the street, very carefully.

LIGHT THE FIRE

Such jolly fun to rake the leaves (Make raking motion with arms)
And see the pile grow higher (Continue raking)
But always wait 'til Daddy comes (Shake right forefinger)
Before you light the fire. (Continue shaking forefinger)

STOOD UP DANGEROUSLY

Silly little Teddy Bear
Stood up in a rocking chair. (Make rocking movement)
Now he has to stay in bed (Lay head on hands)
With a bandage 'round his head. (Circular movement of hand about head)

FALLEN ELECTRICAL WIRE

Here are the poles (Hold forearms and wrists straight vertically)
And here is the wire. (Trace outline of wire suspended between fingertips
with one hand, and resume position)
I'm safe 'cause I'm short and they're so much higher.
But if they've fallen on the ground (Forearms collapse, cross, ending
up horizontal)
I **never** touch, and I walk around.

THE DOOR AND THE DRAWER

When I'm about to close the door, (Hand on doorknob)
Or getting set to shut a drawer, (Hand on drawer knob)
I'm safe by keeping hands and feet (Wave each in turn)
Away from where the surfaces meet. (Point out pinch points, where door
meets jamb and drawer meets table)

82

LOOK BOTH WAYS

Step on the corner
Watch for the light.
Look to the left,
Look to the right.
If nothing is coming
Then start and don't talk
Go straight across
Be careful and walk.

CORNER

Little Jack Horner stood on the corner (Stand with feet together)
Watching the traffic go by (Look to left and right)
And when it passed, he crossed at last (Take two steps forward)
And said, "What a safe boy am I." (Thumbs under arms)

AT THE CURB

At the curb before I cross,
I stop my running feet. (Point to feet)
And look both ways to left and right
Before I cross the street,
Lest autos running quietly
Might come as a surprise.
I don't just listen with my ears, (Point to ears)
But look with both my eyes. (Point to eyes)

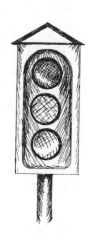

WALKING HOME

When I walk home from school today,
I'll walk the safe and careful way.
I'll look to the left — I'll look to the right.
Then cross the street when no car is in sight.

TRAFFIC LIGHTS

Do you know what traffic lights say to you?
Do you know what traffic lights say to do?
Yellow says, "Be careful" (Hold arm straight out)
Green says, "You may go." (Lower arm)
But red is most important, (Raise arm up)
It says, "Stop?" you know.

WATCH OUT FOR SUNBURN

If your skin is white, or freckled, or pale,
And now you have bright, sunny days,
Wear a light shirt to cover your skin
To protect from the sun's burning rays.

FIVE LITTLE FLAGS

Five little flags were waving in the breeze (One hand up)
And it's these five flags
That the wind likes to tease
For it tosses them up (Fingers flutter up)
And it tosses them down. (Fingers flutter down)
Before it decides
To move swiftly along. (Hand moves swiftly along)

TEN LITTLE SOLDIERS

Ten little soldiers stand in a row (Both hands up, pointers extended)
They all bow down to the captain so! (Bend fingers down and up)
They march to the left, they march to the right. (Move hands to left and then to right)
They stand in a line all ready to fight! (Make two fists)
Then comes the captain with a great big gun. (Pointer fingers extended, thumbs up!)
Bang! Went the gun and away they did run! (Clap hands, wiggle fingers and drop hands into lap)

MY SOLDIERS

My soldiers all in a row. (Ten fingers up straight)
They do not know where to go. (Same)
Along came a man with a gun. (Clap hands together)
My how my soldiers did run! (Both hands behind back)

BEAT THE DRUM

Boom, boom, (Clap hands on each ''Boom'')
Beat the drum.
Boom, boom,
Here we come,
Boom, boom,
Do not lag.
Boom, boom,
Wave the flag. (Flag is four fingers on one hand together, thumb resting on palm)

TEN JOLLY SAILOR BOYS

Ten jolly sailor boys (Both hands up)
Dressed in blue.
Looking at me. (Turn hands towards face)
Looking at you. (Turn hands toward partner's face)

TRANSPORTATION
CHOO-CHOO TRAIN

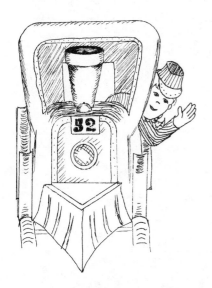

This is a choo-choo train (Bend arms at elbows)
Puffing down the track. (Rotate forearms in rhythm)
Now it's going forward, (Push arms forward; continue rotating motion)
Now the bell is ringing, (Pull bell cord with closed fist)
Now the whistle blows, (Hold fist near mouth and blow)
What a lot of noise it makes. (Cover ears with hands)
Everywhere it goes.

TRAIN

The train's big wheels go clickety-clack (Make circular motions)
As they choo-choo over the railroad track. (Make circular motions over
opposite outstretched arm)

It'll never get lost through thick and thin
For a train only goes where it's already been.

CLICK-CLACK

Click-Clack, Click-Clack (Place elbow on desk and swing arm)
Back and forth, forth and back
Wiper works with might and main
To keep the windshield free from rain.

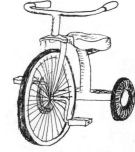

IF I WERE A TRAIN

If I were a choo-choo train.
I'd run along a track.
I'd blow my whistle. (Hand closed like pulling whistle) Toot! Toot!
And let out steam. (Make sound with mouth) Sh . . . Sh . . .
As I go clickety-clack, clickety-clack, clickety-clack.

TOOT AND CHUG

Toot said the little boat sailing along.
Chug, chug, said the little train. "I'm very strong."
Zoom, zoom, said the airplane as he flew away.
But, "Look at me, I can **jump** today." (Hop, skip, run)

MY LITTLE TRICYCLE

My little tricycle has wheels so fine. (Sit on chair)
One in front (Touch wheel in front) and two behind. (Touch wheels on
either side.

I steer in the front from left to right (Do so)
And I ride so fast I'm out of sight. (Pedal rapidly)

DAD'S MOTORCYCLE

My dad has a motorcycle
Sometimes he gives me a ride.
The wind blows my hair,
And oh what a noise,
But I have fun waving to girls and boys.

HERE IS A CAR

Here is a car, shiny and bright. (Cup one hand and place on other palm)
This is the windshield that lets in the light. (Hands open, fingertips touching)
Here are wheels that go round and round (Two fists)
I sit in the back seat and make not a sound. (Sit quietly)

THE CAR RIDE

(Left arm, held out bent, is "road"; right fist is "car")

"Vroom!" says the engine (Place "car" on left shoulder)
As the driver starts the car. (Shake "car")
"Mmm," say the windows
As the driver takes it far. (Travel over upper arm)
" Errrr," says the tires
As it rounds the final bend, (Turn at elbow; proceed over forearm)
"Ahh," says the driver
As his trip comes to an end. (Stop car on left flattened palm)

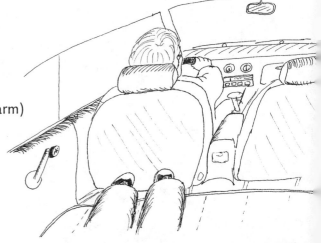

HOW DO I GET FROM HERE TO THERE?

How do I get from here to there? (Scratch head in puzzlement)
If I were a bird, I'd fly through the air. (Flap arms)
How do I get to a mountain peak? (Scratch head in puzzlement)
If I were a snake, I'd slither and sneak. (Move shoulders and body in slithering motion)
How do I get to the merry-go-round? (Scratch head in puzzlement)
If I were a horse, I'd run on the ground. (Stoop, "run" with arms and legs)
How do I get to the candy shop? (Scratch head in puzzlement)
If I were a frog, I'd hop, hop, hop. (Do so, on each "hop")
How do I get to Snickersnee? (Scratch head in puzzlement)
If I were a fish, I'd swim through the sea. (Make swimming motions with arms)

RIDING IN A WAGON

Riding in a wagon (Arm bent at elbows, forearms circling)
Riding in a wagon
Wheels go round and round and round
Riding in a wagon.

SCHOOL BUS

I go to the bus stop each day (Walk one hand across table)
Where the bus comes to take us away. (Stop; have other hand wait too)
We stand single file (One behind the other)
And walk down the aisle. (Step up imaginary steps onto bus)
When the bus driver talks, we obey.

MY AIRPLANE RIDE

We went to the airport to board our plane. (Hand makes swooping motion)
To go away and come back again.
The car was parked and we took the little bus. (Body makes bouncing motions)
We were early so we didn't rush.

As we walked along the airport hall.
We saw the airplanes through big windows in the wall. (Pointer fingers form square)
Big planes, small planes, all in a row. (Hands spread apart horizontally)
The pilots were waiting for their turn to go. (Hands move a pretend wheel)

Many, many people I could see.
Tall ones, short ones, some the same as me. (Right hand up, left hand down,
                                               right pointer points to self)

Our plane was now ready for the flight.
I thought it was the biggest one in sight.

It was time for the passengers to board. (Point to watch or clock)
And it wasn't long before we soared. (Right hand upward sweep)
I was sitting in an airplane seat.
For a little person it was really neat.

I wanted to sit so straight and tall.
So people wouldn't know I was small. (Sit up straight with shoulders back)
I'm sure people knew it was a big person's seat.
Because they could see by my dangling feet. (Move feet back and forth)

So up in the airplane, oh so high.
Flew our airplane into the sky. (Hands up high)
Through the wind and with the sun.
Faster than a horse can run. (Hands hit knees)

Sitting in our seats so still.
Flying over the tallest hill. (Hands up touching)
To a city so far away we could fly in less than a day.
Oh, it's fun to fly! (Arms outstretched)

IF I WERE AN AIRPLANE

If I were an airplane, (Extend arms from shoulder, hold up)
Flying way up high.
I'd tip my wings, (Bend body, one arm up the other down)
To make a turn.
As I go zooming by. (Make zooming sound)

MY BICYCLE

My bicycle is shiny and new (Move hands in a circular motion at sides, as
                                if pedaling a bicycle.)
I like to ride with my friends, do you?
Sometimes we ride fast
Sometimes we ride slow
But we are always careful, you know?

87

math concepts

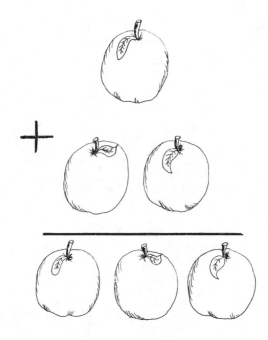

ONE, TWO

(Child stands and follows directions)

One

Show me one hand
Show me one finger
Wiggle one nose
Touch one arm
Shake one head
Sit one body down.

Two

Show me two hands
Wiggle two fingers
Shake two arms
Touch two eyes
Cover two ears
But sit one body down.

HOW MANY . . ?

(Children should respond with proper quantity of fingers)

How many eyes, and how many ears,
And how many noses have I?
How many shoes am I wearing today,
And how many toes have I?
How many sisters and how many dads,
And how many brothers have I?
How many grammas and grampas,
And how many mothers have I?
How many cats, and how many dogs,
And how many pets have I?
How much do I weigh, how tall am I,
And how many years old am I?

TWO LITTLE DICKY BIRDS

Two little dicky birds sitting on a wall (Fingers horizontal thumbs
standing up)
One named Peter, the other named Paul. (Wiggle thumbs as named)
Fly away, Peter, fly away Paul. (Flutter hands behind back)
Come back Peter, come back Paul. (Bring hands back as before)

FIVE LITTLE BIRDS

Five little birds without any home (Hold up five fingers)
Five little trees in a row (Raise hands high over head)
Come build your nests in our branches tall (Cup hands)
We'll rock them to and fro. (Rock nest)

READY FOR SCHOOL

Two little houses closed up tight (Fists closed up thumbs in)
Open up the windows and let in the light (Fingers open)
Ten little finger people tall and straight (Palms to front, fingers erect)
Ready for school at half past eight. (Fingers erect, hands and arms move
forward)

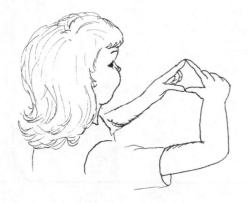

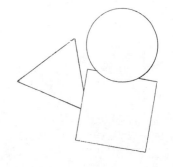

SIMPLE PLANE GEOMETRY

One straight finger makes a line, (Hold up one index finger)
Two straight lines make one "t" sign. (Cross index fingers)
Three lines make a triangle there, (Form triangle with indexes
touching and thumbs touchin
And one more line will make a square. (Form square with hand

90

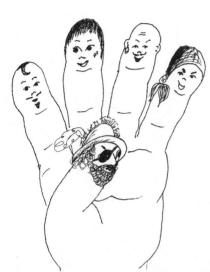

CAPTAIN AND HIS MEN

One, two, three, four, five in a row. (Pop up fingers one at a time
           on right hand)

A captain and his men!
And on the other side, you know,
Are six, seven, eight, nine, ten. (Pop up fingers one at a time on
           left hand)

HERE IS A BALL

Here's a ball (Make circle with thumb and pointer)
And here's a ball (Make circle with two thumbs and pointers)
And a great big ball I see. (Make circle with arms)
Now let's count the balls we've made,
One, two, three. (Repeat as above)

3-D GEOMETRY

A basketball is round and hard, (Pretend to dribble)
Its shape is called a sphere. (Form snowball with hands)
A dice's shape is called a cube,
For its faces are even and clear. (Form cube with hands)

RIGHT CIRCLE, LEFT SQUARE

Close my eyes, shut them tight.
Make a circle with my right.
Keep them shut, make it fair,
With my left hand, make a square.

LITTLE PUSSIES

One, two, three, four. (Hold up four fingers of left hand, touch each one)
One, two, three, four.
These little pussies came to my door.
They just stood there (Fingers straight)
And said, "Good-day". (Bend fingers together)
And then they tiptoed away. (Move fingers behind back)

ME

I have five fingers on each hand. (Point to each body part as it is named)
Ten toes on both feet;
Two ears, two eyes, one nose, mouth
With which to gently speak.
My hands can clap.
My feet can tap.
My eyes can brightly shine.
My ears can hear.
My nose can smell.
My mouth can make a rhyme.

TEN LITTLE FINGERS

I have ten little fingers and ten little toes. (Children point to portions
of body as they repeat words)

Two little arms and one little nose.
One little mouth and two little ears.
Two little eyes for smiles and tears.
One little head and two little feet.
One little chin, that's (Child's name) complete.

LEARN TO COUNT

One, two, three and four;
I can count even more.
Five, six, seven, eight;
See my fingers standing straight, (Raise one finger at a time as you count)
Nine and ten are my thumb men. (Raise thumbs)

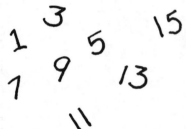

EVENS

If I start with number zero, (Hold up right fist)
And jumped to two, I'd be a hero. (Raise right pinkie and ring; touch
ring with left index)
And four and six and eight and ten (Raise fingers accordingly; six, eight,
and ten should be on left hand, touched
by right index)
And then I'd start it all again. (Hold up right fist alone)

ODDS

If I start with number one, (Hold up right pinkie, touch with left index)
And skip the next one, just for fun, (Bring up right ring and middle fingers;
touch middle)
I'd land on number three, then skip
To five and seven and nine, then quit. (Raise fingers accordingly; seven and
nine displayed on left hand, touched
by right index)

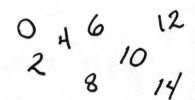

I CAN COUNT

I can count. Want to see?
Here's my fingers. One, two, three. (Hold up one hand, count fingers
with other hand)
Four and five. This hand is done.
Now I'll count the other one.
Six, seven, eight and nine. (Using other hand continue counting)
Just one more. I'm doing fine.
The last little finger is number ten.
Now I'll count them all again.
One, Two, Three, Four, Five, Six, Seven, Eight, Nine, Ten. (Hold fingers Up)

nursery rhymes

JACK AND JILL

Jack and Jill went up the hill (Motion of two fingers climbing up an arm)
To fetch a pail of water.
Jack fell down (One finger doubled under)
And broke his crown.
And Jill came tumbling after. (Both fingers doubled under)

JACK BE NIMBLE

Jack be nimble, (Hold closed fist with thumb standing)
Jack be quick,
Jack jump over (First hand hops over second)
the candlestick.

TWO BLACK BIRDS

There were two blackbirds
Sitting on a hill, (Hold up both hands, thumbs erect, fingers bent)
The one named Jack, (Wiggle one thumb)
The other named Jill (Wiggle other thumb)
Fly away, Jack! (Bend down one thumb)
Fly away, Jill! (Bend down other thumb)
Come back, Jack! (Raise one thumb erect)
Come back, Jill! (Raise other thumb erect)

PAT A CAKE

Pat a cake, pat a cake, baker's man! (Clap four times in rhythm)
Bake me a cake as fast as you can. (Cup hands)
Pat it, and dot it and mark it with B, (Pantomime this action)
And put it in the oven (Extend both hands)
For Baby and Me. (Point to member of class and then to self)

LITTLE JACK HORNER

Little Jack Horner
Sat in the corner,
Eating his Christmas pie. (Pretend to eat from pie)
He put in his thumb (Pat thumb in pie)
And pulled out a plum, (Pull it out)
And said, "What a good boy am I." (Hold thumb up)

LITTLE BO-PEEP

Little Bo-Peep has lost her sheep, (Hold up both hands with fingers extended)
And can't tell where to find them (Hide hands behind back)
Leave them alone and they'll come home. (Bring hands from behind back and
                                                       hold them up)
Wagging their tails behind them (Wiggle fingers)

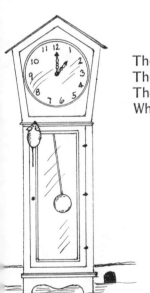

THE OWL

There was an old owl who lived in an oak.
The more he saw, (Point to eyes) the less he spoke. (Cover mouth)
The less he spoke, the more he heard. (Cup hand around ear)
Why can't we be like that wise old bird?

HICKORY DICKORY DOCK

Hickory Dickory Dock (Raise right arm high)
The mouse ran up the clock. (Run fingers of left hand up right arm)
The clock struck one. (Clap hands over head)
The mouse ran down. (Run fingers down arm)
Hickory Dickory Dock.

HERE SITS THE LORD MAYOR

Here sits the Lord Mayor, (Point to forehead)
Here sit his two men: (Point to eyes)
Here sits a rooster, (Point to right cheek)
And here sits a hen. (Point to left cheek)
Here sit the chickens (Point to nose)
Here they run in; (Point to mouth)
Chin-chopper, chin-chopper, (Move chin up and down with fingers)
Chin-chopper, chin!

SING A SONG OF SIXPENCE

Sing a song of sixpence,
A pocket full of rye; (Place hands in imaginary pockets)
Four-and-twenty blackbirds (Flap arms)
Baked in a pie. (Make circle with arms)
When the pie was opened,
The birds began to sing (Two or three children whistle)
Wasn't that a dainty dish
To set before the king?

The king was in the counting house,
Counting out his money. (Motion of piling coins on top of each other)
The queen was in the parlor,
Eating bread and honey (Motion of eating)
The maid was in the garden,
Hanging up the clothes,
When down came a blackbird (Flap arms)
And snipped off her nose. (Pinch nose)

LITTLE MISS MUFFET

Little Miss Muffet sat on a tuffet (Fist with thumb standing)
Eating her curds and whey, (Pretend to eat)
Along came a spider (Running motion with fingers)
And sat down beside her. ("Spider" sits down beside "tuffet")
And frightened Miss Muffet away. (Throw hands out)

LITTLE BOY BLUE

Little Boy Blue, come blow your horn; (Hold up clenched hands in a
make believe horn)
The sheep are in the meadow, (Hold up left hand and bend down fingers)
The cows are in the corn (Hold up right hand and bend down fingers)
Where is the little boy who looks after the sheep? (Spread hands questioningly)
He's under the haystack,
Fast asleep! (Place palms together and lay head to one side on hands)

96

mythology, magic & make-believe

THE SAND DRAGON

Today I was in my sandbox
And I made myself a dragon. ("play" with sand)
I wanted to show it to my mom
So I put it in my wagon. ("lift" dragon and put in wagon)

I pulled it over bumpy grass ("pull" wagon a few steps)
And yelled and waved my hand. (wave hand)
Mom smiled and said, "What dragon, child?" (turn around)
There was nothing there but sand.

LITTLE HUEY DRAGON
(an exercise)

Little Huey Dragon counts to three,
Little Huey Dragon bends one knee.
Little Huey Dragon stretches his wings,
Little Huey Dragon whistles and sings. (la la)
Little Huey Dragon touches his toes,
Little Huey Dragon touches his nose.
Little Huey Dragon makes a funny face,
Little Huey Dragon runs in place.
Little Huey Dragon lays on the floor,
Little Huey Dragon starts to snore.

LITTLE HUEY DRAGON DRESSES UP RIGHT

Little Huey Dragon says, "It's time to go to town." (hands on hips)
Little Huey Dragon dresses up (touch head) to down. (touch feet)
Little Huey Dragon puts on a hat; (place palm on head)
Little Huey Dragon gives his tummy a pat. (pat stomach)
Little Huey Dragon puts on his shirt; (put on invisible shirt)
Little Huey Dragon brushes off some dirt. (brush sleeves, frowning)
Little Huey Dragon wears a tie; (twiddle fingers at throat)
Little Huey Dragon rubs his eye. (rub eye)
Little Huey Dragon steps into his slacks; (step into slacks)
Little Huey Dragon scratches his back. (scratch back)
Little Huey Dragon puts on his shoes and socks; (do so)
Little Huey Dragon doesn't ride, he walks. (walks)

WAIT, WAIT, WAIT A BIT

(sung to the tune of "Row, Row, Row Your Boat")

Wait, wait, wait a bit
Till Wizard's in his hole;
Quietly, quietly, quietly, quietly,
Read the book you stole.

Wave, wave, wave your arms
And whisper magic words;
Noisily, noisily, noisily, noisily,
Stones turn into birds!

"Caw, caw, caw," they screech.
"Give us food to eat!"
Magic word, magic word, magic words, magic words,
Birds change into sheep!

"Baa, baa, baa," they shout, and
Before you can resist,
Angrily, angrily, angrily, angrily,
Wizard grabs your wrist.

Pa-pop, pa-pop, pa-pop, the sheep
Are each turned back to stone;
Sadly, so sadly, so sadly, so sadly,
Now you walk alone.

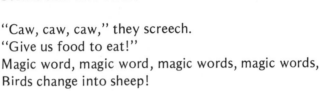

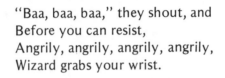

THE HIDER

A beast that takes and hides our stuff (hold up fist; grab fist with
　　　　　　　　　　　　　　　　other hand; hide fist behind back)
Is what we call a hider.
We think it's smaller than a mouse (display fist)
But larger than a spider. (undulate fingers for spider's legs)
No one's ever seen one, but (cover eyes)
We know when he's been near, (look down, hands on hips)
Cuz a shoe or glove or comb or toy
That was there (point far away) is over **here.** (point at feet)

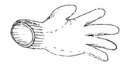

THE GIANT AND THE LEPRECHAUN

There was a little leprechaun (crouch down to indicate short stature)
Whose home was in a tree.
He met a giant in the park (stand straight and tall)
And asked her home for tea. (still standing, curtsey)

They walked inside the tiny house (make opening-door motion)
But the giant broke the door.
She stood up tall and smashed the roof, (bend over, stand up suddenly,
        as if breaking through)
Her feet crashed through the floor! (pick feet up as if wading through mud)

The giant stopped. "Oh, what a mess! (stand up tall, palms to cheeks,
         elbows out in distress)
"I'm very sorry!" she cried. (wipe away tears)
"That's quite all right," said the leprechaun. (crouch down)
"We'll drink our tea outside." (still crouching, make drinking-tea motions)

A PIECE OF STRING

What can I do with a piece of string?
I can lace and tie my shoe.
I can fly a kite and make a knot
Or cut it in half to make two.

What can I do with a piece of string?
I can knot it into a net.
I can play Cat's Cradle or make Jacob's Ladder
Or tie up a wandering pet.

PEGASUS

I am called a Pegasus.
I'm a horse which flies through air.
I was born with wings, you see,
And I fly anywhere!

But that was long ago, my friend,
Our numbers now are few.
You now know of us only as
The horses once that flew.

THE YOUNG MAN FROM THE MOON

There was a young man from the moon
Who visited Earth once in June.
He had so much fun
He missed the Moon-run
And had to get back by balloon.

DAWN AND DAVE

(sung to the tune of "Jack and Jill")

Dawn and Dave hid in a cave
To try and catch a fairy;
Dawn got wet and waved her net
And caught a small canary.

101

PETER HAD A UNICORN

(sung to the tune of "Mary Had A Little Lamb")

Peter had a unicorn, unicorn, unicorn,
Peter had a unicorn whose coat was black as night.

On her head between her ears, 'tween her ears, 'tween her ears,
On her head between her ears her horn was snowy white.

Once as they were on a walk, on a walk, on a walk,
Once as they were on a walk a crabby troll appeared.

It shouted at them, "Go away! Go away! Go away!"
It shouted at them, "Go away!" which was what Peter feared.

But unicorn was not afraid, not afraid, not afraid,
But unicorn was not afraid and toward the troll they sped.

As soon as they were close enough, close enough, close enough,
As soon as they were close enough, she kissed it on the head.

Now the three are best of friends, best of friends, best of friends,
Now the three are best of friends and share their evening bread.

FRANK AND HANK

There once was a centaur named Frank
Who sat next to a demon named Hank.
Said Frank to the demon,
"Let's play we are sea men,"
But when they went sailing they sank.

THE CENTAUR

I am called a centaur,
A field is my home. (bring arm out expansively)
I'm partly man (start hand at waist, move upwards)
    and partly horse (move hand from waist **down**
    and **behind**)
And my best friend is a gnome. (hold index up,
    bend once or twice for gnome)
I'm very smart, for I'm part man, (tap side of head)
I can write (make writing gestures) and read.
    (hold left hand flat to indicate book, run
    right index finger over as if reading)
I'm very strong, for I'm part horse, (flex arms
    to show off muscles)
And I run with super speed. (run in place)

CHESTER AND THE RABBIT

Chester Centaur saw a rabbit (make raking motions)
While working in his garden; (slowly cease raking motions, focus
                     eyes on one spot)
It pawed the ground and looked around (hands behind back,
                     shuffle feet, look around)

And said, "I beg your pardon,
I need to know the way to go
To get to Kalamazoo."
Chester just pointed and the rabbit said, "Thanks
I'll remember a centaur like you." (tip invisible hat)

THE UNICORN

I am called a unicorn.
I look just like a horse.
Except between my ears I have
A spiral horn, of course.

Magic cannot harm me
For I am magic, too.
I come in many different colors
From white to green to blue.

I'm glad that I'm a unicorn
'Cuz I have so much fun!
My horn's a musical instrument
And I play it as I run.

MERMAID

I am called a mermaid.
My home is in the sea. (make swimming motions)
My friends are fish (make pah—pah—pah motions for fish "breathing")
      and whales (spread arms to indicate huge size);
They like to play with me. (indicate self)

I look just like you, my friend, (sweeping gesture to audience)
From navel (point at) to my head (touch top of head),
But I do not have legs like you. (point to each leg, shaking head)
I have flukes instead.   (sitting, bring legs close together,
      point feet splay-footed, and kick)

MILLIE AND THE UNICORN

As Millie the mermaid sat by the beach,
      (splay feet, legs together, sit)
Along came a unicorn just out of reach.
      (seated as above, smile, wave)
"Come here, little fellow. I mean you no harm."
      (hold hand out)
But the unicorn whinnied and ran in alarm.
      (withdraw hand, look disappointed)
Millie thought, "What gave that colt such a scare?
      (scratch head)
I think I'll get rid of this eel in my hair."
      (remove something from head)
A little bit later the unicorn returned,
      (smile, seated as above still, hold out hand)
And gave Millie a ride for which she had yearned.

activity verses

THE CUCKOO CLOCK

I like to watch our cuckoo clock,
And see the little bird.
He makes the funniest sound,
That I have ever heard.
When the clock strikes the hour,
The cuckoo bird pops out.   (Children jump ahead — Bend knees)
He wags his head back and forth,   (Move head back and forth)
And gives this funny shout,
Cuckoo! Cuckoo! Cuckoo!   (Wag head on each cuckoo)

POPCORN

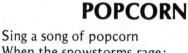

Sing a song of popcorn
When the snowstorms rage;
Fifty little round men
Put into a cage. (Cup hands together, palms in, fingertips touching)
Shake them all — they laugh and leap (Shake cage)
Crowding to the top.
Watch them burst their little coats
Pop! Pop! Pop! (Clap three times)

POP! POP! POP!

Pop! Pop! Pop! (Clap hands)
Pour the corn into the pot.
Pop! Pop! Pop! (Clap hands)
Take and shake it 'til it's hot.
Pop! Pop! Pop! (Clap hands)
Lift the lid — what have we got?
Pop! Pop! Pop! (Clap hands)
POPCORN! (Say loudly)

THE TEAPOT

I'm a little teapot, short and stout
This is my handle (Put one hand on hip)
This is my spout. (Extend opposite arm sideways, hand out)
When I get all steamed up, then I shout
Just tip me over and pour me out. (Bend body toward extended arm)
I'm a very clever pot, it's true.
Here's an example of what I can do.
I can change my handle and change my spout (Change position of hands)
Just tip me over and pour me out. (Bend body in opposite direction)

LITTLE BEAR

Little Bear, Little Bear, turn around (Turn around)
Little Bear, Little Bear, touch the ground (Touch the floor)
Little Bear, Little Bear, climb the stairs (Pretend to climb stairs)
Little Bear, Little Bear, say your prayers (Fold hands)
Little Bear, Little Bear, turn out the light (Pretend to turn off light)
Little Bear, Little Bear, say "Good-night." (Lay head on side of hands)

ZIG-ZAG CHILDREN

I know a little zig-zag boy
Who goes this way and that (Two steps to left, two steps to right)
He never knows just where he puts
His coat or shoes or hat. (Point to shoulders, shoes, head)

I know a little zig-zag girl,
Who flutters here and there (Hands flutter to left and right)
She never knows just where to find
Her brush to fix her hair. (Point to hair)

If you are not a zig-zag child,
You'll have no cause to say
That you forgot, for you will know
Where things are put away.

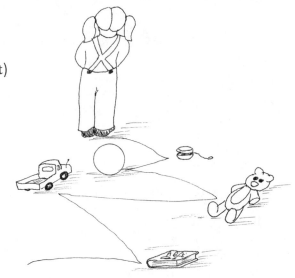

SOMETIMES MY HANDS ARE NAUGHTY

Sometimes my hands are naughty (Slap hand)
And so my mother says
That she will have to scold them,
And send them off to bed. (Close eyes, lay head on hands)
So little hands be careful, please, (Look down at hands)
Of everything you do.
Because if you are sent to bed,
I'll have to go there, too.

BLOWING BUBBLES

It's fun to blow bubbles,
On a bright, sunny day,
And see how they sparkle and shine,
As they float away.

WOODEN WILLIAM

I'm just like Wooden William
Who stands up straight and tall. (Stand stiff and straight)
My arms and legs are wooden (Arms hang rigidly at sides)
They just don't move at all.

A COWBOY

A cowboy wears a western hat,
And rides a frisky horse,
He carries a rope called a lariat,
He's a real straight shooter, of course.

MY MOTHER'S BOUQUET

See the pretty flowers that I picked today. (Make fist like holding flowers)
I'm making my mother a pretty bouquet.
My mother will like this,
They smell pretty, you know. (Sniff flowers — smile at good smell)
I'll give her a hug and say, "I love you, so."

THE BABY

Sh! Be Quiet! (Finger over lips)
The baby is sleeping. (Arms like a cradle rocking a baby)
Sh! Be Quiet! (Finger over lips)
The baby is sleeping. (Arms like cradle rocking a baby)
Sh! Be Quiet! (Finger over lips)
The baby is sleeping. (Arms like cradle, etc.)
We don't want to wake it up.

Walk on tip-toe, (Walking on tip toe)
So we don't make a sound.
Walk on tip-toe,
So we don't make a sound.
Walk on tip-toe,
So we don't make a sound.
Or the baby will start to cry.

The baby woke up,
And is crying waa-waa. (Rub eyes as if crying)
The baby woke up,
And is crying WAA-WAA.
The baby woke up,
And is crying W A A - W A A!
See all the tears on its face. (Use pointer fingers to make tears running down face)

We'll tickle the baby,
Under the chin. (Tickle self under chin)
We'll tickle the baby,
Under the chin.
We'll tickle the baby,
Under the chin.
Maybe the baby will smile.

See how the baby
Starts to grin. (Smile)
See how the baby
Starts to grin.
See how the baby
Starts to grin.
Now we are happy again!

A SMILE

Raise your arms away up high.
Wiggle your fingers at the sky.
Down at your sides. Then jump in place.
Put a smile on your face.

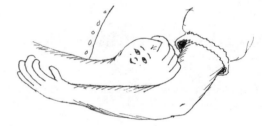

BABY

Here is baby's tousled head (Make a fist)
He nods and nods; (Bend fist back and forth)
Let's put him to bed. (Bend other arm and tuck fist into brook of elbow)

FLOPPY RAG DOLL

I'm a floppy, floppy rag doll, (Sit with head, arms and shoulders drooping)
Drooping in my chair, (Continue relaxed position, head, arms and shoulders drooping, hips well back against chair)
My head just rolls from side to side, (Roll head over to left shoulder then slowly roll it around to fall limply over right shoulder)
My arms fall through the air. (Still sitting, let hands hang completely relaxed over side of chair, and swing very slowly in limp fashion, from shoulder sockets)

HAMMER, HAMMER, HAMMER

Hammer, hammer, hammer, (Pound fist on other palm)
I drive the nails so straight.
Do you know what I'm building?
A truck for hauling freight.
I'm sawing, sawing, sawing (Move hand back and forth on opposite palm)
To make my wheels go round;
I nail my truck together
Pound, pound, pound. (Pound fist on opposite palm)

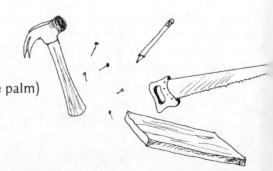

CIRCLE GAMES

HOP AND TWIRL

Make a circle and we'll go around.
First walk on tip-toe so we don't make a sound.
Tip, toe, around we go.
Then hop on our left foot, and then on our right.
Then hop together. What a funny sight!
Now stop hopping and twirl around.
Now we're ready to settle down.

STAND IN A CIRCLE

Stand in a circle and clap your hands.
Clap, clap, clap, clap.
Now put your hands over your head.
Slap, slap, slap, slap.
Now hands at your sides and turn around.
Then in our circle we'll all sit down.

A CIRCLE

Around in a circle we will go.
Little tiny baby steps,
Make us go very slow.
And then we'll take some great giant steps,
As big as they can be.
Then in our circle we'll stand quietly.

1 TO 10 CIRCLE

Let's make a circle and around we go.
Not too fast and not too slow.
One, two, three, four, five, — six, seven, eight, nine, ten.
Let's face the other way and go around again.
One, two, three, four, five, — six, seven, eight, nine, ten.

THE LOST PRINCE

A long time ago in a far away place
There was a little town.
Within the town's castle upon her throne,
The worried queen sat with a frown.

"Where is the King?" she asked of the Duke.
"Has he found our little son?"
"Fear not, Your Highness," assured the Duke.
"The search has only just begun."

Deep in the woods surrounding the town
The King stood in a glen.
His army watched near, and the King cleared his throat,
And he called out to all of his men;

"My son has strayed off of the playing-ground."
His voice rose to a shout.
"We must find him soon, before nightfall,
Before the Beast comes out!"

Now, no one had ever seen the Beast
Or no one had lived to tell.
But enormous paw-prints were discovered nearby
And they feared it did not mean well.

The men split up and searched the woods
And called till their throats were dry;
"Young prince! Come out, wherever you are!"
While the sun sank lower in the sky.

The search finally quit as the stars lit the sky
For the men feared the Beast by night.
They'd heard bloody tales of sharp teeth and claws
And the horrible Beast's love to fight.

"This night drags on endlessly," whispered the King,
As he heard the Beast's howls outside.
The King and Queen hugged, and went to bed.
Neither one slept, though they tried.

Though the dark night was laden with grief and despair,
The morning brought unbounded joy;
For into the playing-ground, just as he left,
All laughing and smiles, came their boy!

"My son! Oh, my darling!" the happy Queen cried.
"Thank God! You do not seem hurt.
You naughty, bad boy, where have you been?
And what is this thing on your shirt?"

For a note was pinned to the small boy's sleeve,
As she read, the Queen's smile increased;
"I believe I've found someone of yours."
It was signed, "Your friend, the Beast."

COLOR GAME

(Teacher should have tag board in the following colors: red, yellow, green, blue, orange, brown, purple. Pass out colors so each child has a colored piece of tag board.)

We can play a color game.
Here's the colors we can name.
Red, yellow, green, and blue.
There's orange and brown,
And purple, too.
Hold up the red card,
Raise it high.
Now hold up yellow
To the sky.
Then hold up the card that's blue,
Now orange, then brown,
And purple, too.
Now put down the card that's blue.
Then yellow, red and purple, too.
Now the colors green, orange and brown.
Now all the colors should be down.

PARTNER GAME

Pick a partner. Take their hand.
Then in a circle partners stand.
Take two steps forward,
And two steps back.
Then bow to your partner
And clap, clap, clap.
Wrap your elbows
And around you go.
Not too fast and not too slow.
Change elbows.
Go around again.
Then stand in a circle
And count to ten.

JACK IN A BOX

If I were a Jack-in-a-box,
I'd make myself very small.
I'd be shut tight inside my box.
You couldn't see me at all. (Crouch way down)

Until someone turns the crank,
The music will play — then stop,
The top will fly open,
And out I'll pop! (Jump up, raise arms up)

JACK-IN-THE-BOX

Jack-in-the-box all shut up tight. (Fingers wrapped around thumb)
Not a breath of air, not a ray of light. (Other hand covers fist)
How tired we must be all down in a heap. (Lift off)
I'll open the lid and up you will leap. (Thumb pops up)

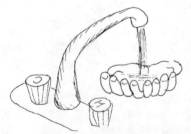

I CAN MAKE A HAMMOCK

I can make a hammock, (Lock fingers, palms up)
I can make a cup. (Cup hands)
Here's the way to make a ball (Fingers and thumbs touch for circle)
Here's how I toss it up! (Tossing motion)

THIS IS A CHURCH

This is the church (Fingers interlocked, palms together)
This is the steeple (Two pointer fingers up to form steeple)
This is the bell (Fingers interlocked and palms together)
That calls to the people. (Rock hands back and forth like pealing bell)
This is a chair (Right fingertips bent and touching left palm)
And this is a piano (Move fingers as if playing piano)
That plays a sweet air.

THE MAGIC WAND

You get a present in the mail
But do not know who wrote.
You open the box and see inside
A magic wand and note.

You get a drink and stare a bit
At the magic stick you've found.
You accidentally knock over the glass
To form a puddle on the ground.

Just for fun, you start to play
And wave your magic wand.
The puddle that the water made
Then grows into a pond.

You think, "Hey, that's a super trick!"
And give the wand a shake.
Too late, you notice that the pond
Has turned into a lake.

"It's getting deep!" you realize
And swim toward a tree.
While climbing up, you drop the wand,
And the lake swells into a sea.

You're scared to death you've lost the wand
'Til you see a bobbing motion,
You dive and swim to get the stick
And the sea becomes an ocean!

You're getting tired, you've lost all hope
But you gather strength and cry,
"I wish I'd read the directions first!"
And suddenly, you're dry!

The ocean's gone, but the puddle remains.
Wand and note are beside your toes,
The note says, "When you wave this wand,
Whate'er's beneath it grows."

MUSICAL INSTRUMENTS

This is how a horn sounds;
Toot! Toot! Toooo! (Play imaginary trombone or trumpet)

This is how guitars sound;
V-rrr-oom, v-rooom, v-rrr-rooo. (Strum imaginary guitar; roll r's)

This is how pianos sound;
Tinkle, grumble, brr-ing! (Run fingers over imaginary keyboard)

This is how a drum sounds;
Bimble, buff, bing! (Strike imaginary drum set, including cymbol)

THE NUT THAT SCOTT FOUND

This is the nut that Scott found. (Separate index and thumb by small
amount to indicate size)
This is the tree (Hold arms out as if tree)
That grew from the nut that Scott found. (Separate index and thumb)

This is the bird (Flap arms)
That sang in the tree (Hold arms out)
That grew from the nut that Scott found. (Separate index and thumb)

This is the minstrel (Play imaginary recorder)
That heard the bird (Flap arms)
That sang in the tree (Hold arms out)
That grew from the nut that Scott found. (Separate index and thumb)

This is the crowd (Clap enthusiastically)
That applauded the minstrel (Play imaginary recorder)
That heard the bird (Flap arms)
That sang in the tree (Hold arms out)
That grew from the nut that Scott found. (Separate index and thumb)

This is the guard with the mole on his chin (Point at chin)
That broke up the crowd (Clap)
That applauded the minstrel (Play imaginary recorder)
That heard the bird (Flap arms)
That sang in the tree (Hold arms out)
That grew from the nut that Scott found. (Separate index and thumb)

This is the mistress of needle and pin (Make sewing motions)
That married the guard with the mole on his chin (Point at chin)
That broke up the crowd (Clap)
That applauded the minstrel (Play imaginary recorder)
That heard the bird (Flap arms)
That sang in the tree (Hold arms out)
That grew from the nut that Scott found. (Separate index and thumb)

This is the cave, so dark within (Cover eyes)
That frightened the mistress of needle and pin (Make sewing motions)
That married the guard with the mole on his chin (Point at chin)
That broke up the crowd (Clap)
That applauded the minstrel (Play imaginary recorder)
That heard the bird (Flap arms)
That sang in the tree (Hold arms out)
That grew from the nut that Scott found. (Separate index and thumb)

This is the girl with the sly little grin (Little girl stance; clasp hands
                                            behind back, smile shyly, turn
                                            face so cheek touches a shoulder)
That entered the cave, so dark within (Cover eyes)
That frightened the mistress of needle and pin (Make sewing motions)
That married the guard with the mole on his chin (Point at chin)
That broke up the crowd (Clap)
That applauded the minstrel (Play imaginary recorder)
That heard the bird (Flap arms)
That sang in the tree (Hold arms out)
That grew from the nut that Scott found. (Separate index and thumb)

This is the dragon with scaly skin (Make terrible face, bring arms up
                                      as if about to attack, or scratch)
That played with the girl with the sly little grin (Little girl stance)
That entered the cave, so dark within (Cover eyes)
That frightened the mistress of needle and pin (Make sewing motions)
That married the guard with the mole on his chin (Point at chin)
That broke up the crowd (Clap)
That applauded the minstrel (Play imaginary recorder)
That heard the bird (Flap arms)
That sang in the tree (Hold arms out)
That grew from the nut that Scott found. (Separate index and thumb)

(Flop down and catch your breath – you've finished!)

ADDITIONAL FAVORITES

ADDITIONAL FAVORITES